RAND ARROYO CENTER

T0288865

Developing a National Recruiting Difficulty Index

Jeffrey B. Wenger, David Knapp, Parag Mahajan, Bruce R. Orvis, Tiffany Tsai

Prepared for the United States Army

For more information on this publication, visit www.rand.org/t/RR2637

Library of Congress Cataloging-in-Publication Data is available for this publication.
ISBN: 978-1-9774-0190-8

Published by the RAND Corporation, Santa Monica, Calif.
© Copyright 2019 RAND Corporation
RAND® is a registered trademark.

Support RAND
Make a tax-deductible charitable contribution at
www.rand.org/giving/contribute

www.rand.org

Preface

This report documents research and analysis conducted as part of a project entitled *Developing a National Recruiting Difficulty Index*, sponsored by U.S. Army Recruiting Command and the Deputy Chief of Staff, G-1, U.S. Army. The purpose of the project was to develop a national recruiting difficulty index that provides an empirically defensible basis to communicate with senior Army leadership regarding future recruiter requirements, advertising budget requirements, enlistment incentive budget requirements, and the needed distribution of other limited resources.

The Project Unique Identification Code (PUIC) for the project that produced this document is RAN167281.

This research was conducted within RAND Arroyo Center's Personnel, Training, and Health Program. RAND Arroyo Center, part of the RAND Corporation, is a federally funded research and development center (FFRDC) sponsored by the United States Army.

RAND operates under a "Federal-Wide Assurance" (FWA00003425) and complies with the *Code of Federal Regulations for the Protection of Human Subjects Under United States Law* (45 CFR 46), also known as "the Common Rule," as well as with the implementation guidance set forth in U.S. Department of Defense (DoD) Instruction 3216.02. As applicable, this compliance includes reviews and approvals by RAND's Institutional Review Board (the Human Subjects Protection Committee) and by the U.S. Army. The views of sources utilized in this study are solely their own and do not represent the official policy or position of DoD or the U.S. government.

Contents

Figures and Tables

Figures

Tables

Summary

The Army has long recognized that the recruiting environment has a significant impact on its ability to recruit. Successfully achieving a mission goal of 80,000 annual recruits is tremendously more difficult when the national unemployment rate is 4 percent than when it is 9 percent. Additionally, when casualty rates increase or operational difficulties mount, recruiting difficulty worsens. The Army may even experience a recruiting mission failure before it systematically reprograms resources. To prevent future recruiting mission failures and allow sufficient time to reprogram resources in the most cost-effective way, the Army requires some advance warning of impending or existing recruiting difficulty. To that end, the RAND Arroyo Center has built a forecasting model that provides a measure of the recruiting difficulty with up to a 24-month horizon.

The recruiting difficulty index (RDI) model consists of seven equations. Three of the equations are for outcomes reflecting recruiting difficulty, and four equations are related to the recruiting process and reflect decisions made by the Army in an ongoing effort to meet recruiting targets. The outcomes for recruiting difficulty are the *percentage* difference between signed enlistment contracts for high school diploma graduates with an Armed Forces Qualification Test (AFQT) score of 50 or higher ("graduate alphas") and the contract mission for them; the average amount of time in the Delayed Entry Pool (DEP; i.e., the average number of days between signing a contract and being accessed into the Army); and the training seat fill rate. Recruiting difficulty is indicated when contracts fall short of the mission goal. By using the percentage shortfall, the approach avoids differences in the scale of the recruiting mission. Recruiting difficulty is also indicated by a low average number of days in the DEP, implying that the DEP pool has been drained to meet accession and training intake requirements, and by training seat fill rate (i.e., a high vacancy rate means that training seats are unfilled because there are too few accessions). The four equations reflecting the Army's response to recruiting conditions are for quick-ship bonuses (a bonus to access into the Army very quickly), military occupational specialty (MOS) enlistment bonuses (higher bonuses are needed when recruiting for a given MOS is more difficult), the number of recruiters on duty (duty recruiters are the individuals that find, inform, and persuade prospects to enlist), and the use of conduct waivers. In addition, the seven equations include variables exogenous to the Army that reflect economic conditions, geopolitical risks, and deployment-related injury and death rates. The data are monthly for fiscal years 2003 through 2015. Data from 2016 were used for out-of-sample model validation (that is, comparing the forecast values to the observed values for 2016) and, subsequently, included for forecasts through FY 2018.

The model's structure is as follows. First, the exogenous variables can affect all seven outcome variables. Second, the policy response variables—quick-ship bonuses, MOS bonuses, duty recruiters, and conduct waivers—can be entered as explanatory variables in the equations indicating recruiting difficulty (in terms of the percentage difference between graduate-alpha contracts and mission, average months in DEP, and training seat fill rate). Third, the criterion of mean-squared prediction error (MSPE) is used when estimating the model in deciding which variables to include as explanatory variables in each equation and whether lagged values of the dependent variables should be included in the explanatory variables (and, if so, how many lags).

One difficulty in building forecast models is having a method to assess whether a variable belongs in a model. Here we use an objective, meaningful method for determining whether to include a variable. The method is based on Hansen (2010) and the process of estimation results in equation specifications and estimates that minimize the prediction errors of the model for the data set to which it is applied. This is an ideal criterion for a model intended for near-term prediction.

Because the variety of possible equation specifications is enormous, we combine prior research, economic theory, and individual judgment in building the model.

Our approach was implemented in three phases of estimation. In the first phase, the equations include a fixed, starter set of exogenous variables; many variants of lagged endogenous variables were tried until there was no further decrease in mean-squared forecast error (MSFE). The number of lags tried was limited to one or two. In phase two, the lagged endogenous variables from phase one were held constant and many variants of the exogenous variables were tried until there was no further improvement in MSFE. Finally, in phase three, the included exogenous variables from phase two were held constant, and again many variants of lagged endogenous variables were included—this time allowing for more lags. Often, two or three lags were selected and more "cross-lags" were entered—for example, the alpha contracts equations included two lags in DEP length as well as many other lagged variables. In effect, phases one and two were a screening process that sought promising candidate exogenous variables and lagged endogenous variables, and the third phase provided by far the greatest improvement in MSFE. Because the third phase allowed for more and longer lags of the endogenous variables than in the first phase, the greatly decreased MSFE in the third phase can be interpreted as resulting from predictive information supplied by the additional lags. This implies that the recruiting system had considerable inertia, and the multiplicity of recruiting-related outcomes contained a good deal of information about recruiting difficulty—lags in DEP length, conduct waivers, quick-ship bonuses, and recruiters on duty all entered the final specification of the alpha contracts equation, for instance.

Overall, model fit was excellent, as can be seen in Figure S.1. In this figure, we used our final model specification and data from 2003 to 2012 to estimate the initial model parameters. Then we estimate a 12-month step ahead forecast (green). Each point on the green line was forecasted using all the data one year prior to the forecast. For example, the forecast for January 2012 was made using data from January 2003 to January 2011. The blue line is the forecast for FY 2016 without the benefit of having realized any FY 2016 data. In general, the in-sample

Figure S.1
Empirical Performance and Current Forecast: (Contracts – Contract Mission)/ (Contract Mission) for Graduate Alpha

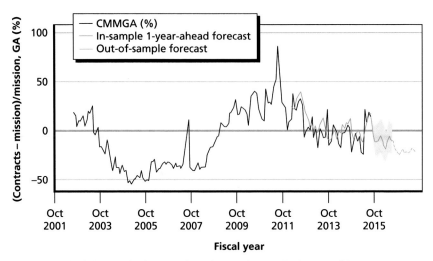

NOTE: The black line in the figure is based on authors' calculations of (contracts – contract mission) / (contract mission) for graduate alphas, using data from the U.S. Army Recruiting Command (USAREC) missioning database and the Regular Army Analyst file. The green line represents a 12-month recursive forecast using the optimized forecast model from January 2012 to September 2015. The solid blue line represents a 1- to 12-month out-of-sample forecast for fiscal year 2016, where the top and bottom bounds of the shaded region reflect the 95 percent confidence interval. The dashed line represents a 13- to 24-month out-of-sample forecast for fiscal year 2017. The forecast for FY 2017 is focused on the recruiting environment and does not account for the mission increase of 6,000 accessions that occurred during FY 2017.

forecast (green) was quite close to the actual realization of the data one year later (black). As we show in the main body of the text, the out-of-sample forecasts did a very good job of predicting the actual outcomes. Using the same ideas, we extend the forecast horizon to 24 months. Those results are shown in the dotted blue line in Figure S.1.

Figure S.1 shows the performance of the forecasting model for one of our key outcomes (contracts − contract mission) / (contract mission) for graduate alphas. The most current forecast shows a difficult recruiting environment—one where the number of contracts written is lower than the contract mission.

Acknowledgments

Many people contributed their talents and insight into the development of the National Recruiting Difficulty Index. A number of senior staff from Army G-1, U.S. Army Recruiting Command, and the Army Marketing Research Group raised a number of important issues regarding data quality and model interpretation as well as providing additional insights about other potential factors that might lead to changes in the recruiting environment. At RAND, Michael Shanley assisted us with the Army Training Requirements and Resources System (ATRRS) data; and Shanthi Nataraj and Michael Hansen provided critical feedback about the model. James Hosek of RAND, and Matthew Goldberg of the Institute for Defense Analyses, provided detailed expert reviews on an early draft of this document and provided important insights about how to clarify and organize the exposition.

Abbreviations

AFQT	Armed Forces Qualification Test
AIC	Akaike Information Criterion
AIT	Advanced Individual Training
AMRG	Army Marketing Research Group
AP	Associated Press
ATRRS	Army Training Requirements and Resources System
AVF	All-Volunteer Force
BAH	Basic Allowance Housing
BCT	Basic Combat Training
CMMGA	(Contracts – Contract Mission)/(Contract Mission), Graduate Alpha
CV	Cross validation
DEP	Delayed Entry Program
DMDC	Defense Manpower Data Center
DoD	U.S. Department of Defense
FFRDC	Federally Funded Research and Development Center
FRED	Federal Reserve Economic Data
GA	Graduate alpha

GED	general equivalency diploma
GPR	Geopolitical Risk
HRC	U.S. Army Human Resources Command
IET	Initial Entry Training
MOS	Military Occupational Specialty
MSFE	Mean-squared forecast error
MSPE	Mean-squared prediction error
NPS	Nonprior Service
OSUT	One Station Unit Training
PCA	Principal component analysis
PUIC	Project unique identification code
QS	Quick-ship
RA	Regular Army
RCM	Recruiting Contract Month
RDI	Recruiting Difficulty Index
RMSE	Root mean-squared error
RRM	Recruiting Resource Model
RSID	Recruiting Centers Identification Designator
RSM	Recruiting Ship Month
SIC	Schwarz Information Criterion
SOOS PMFE	Pseudo-out-of-sample predicted mean forecast error
TRADOC	U.S. Training and Doctrine Command
TSFR	Training Seat Fill Rate
UMCSENT	University of Michigan Consumer Sentiment
USAREC	U.S. Army Recruiting Command

CHAPTER ONE

Introduction

Background

Recruiting resources have historically been programmed largely based on the size of the recruiting mission and less so by recruiting market difficulty. One potential consequence is that recruiting resources can be insufficient when the recruiting environment is difficult and overly abundant during periods of easier recruiting. This mismatch is often difficult to correct because (a) providing an assessment of the recruiting environment (either qualitatively or quantitatively) is difficult; and (b) forecasting changes in the recruiting environment means modeling not only macroeconomic and geopolitical risks, but also Army responses to perceived recruiting success/failure. Typically, recruiting failure is the tipping point that leads to increasing recruiting resources and a strong indicator of recruiting difficulty. The unemployment rate is often used as a more nuanced proxy for recruiting difficulty, but the unemployment rate alone has not been a sufficient signal to reprogram resources. In part, this is because unemployment is only part of the reason for a difficult recruiting environment. General economic and world conditions, enlistment propensity, and the demographics of potential recruits combine with specific recruiting goals to make the job of recruiting relatively harder or easier each year.

Currently, there are only limited metrics of recruiting difficulty, and the relationship between these metrics and required resourcing for a recruiting mission is not well understood. Many of the Army's recruiting tools (e.g., recruiters, advertising campaigns) take time to develop in order to become fully productive. Therefore, the Army needs to understand more fully the primary factors in recruiting difficulty, how much each factor accounts for variation in recruiting difficulty, and the relationships among the factors and conditions that influence them. A national recruiting difficulty index would enable the Army to assess the extent to which recruiting difficulty has changed over time, predict the level of difficulty in future years, and communicate future periods of potential difficulty, thereby providing planners time to sufficiently resource the recruiting mission.

Purpose of the Report

This report provides a review of the existing literature to identify the extent to which economic factors, recruiting mission, Delayed Entry Program (DEP) posture, enlistment eligibility policies, propensity, recruiting resources, and world/Army events associated with public perceptions of the conditions of service have been shown or posited to negatively/positively affect recruiting difficulty. Based on information developed in the literature review, discussions with resource planners, and additional, quantitative analyses, RAND Arroyo Center built a conceptual model of direct and indirect influences on desirable/adverse recruiting outcomes. Based on the conceptual model, the research team built an empirical model that provides recruiting difficulty forecasts for up to 24 months into the future. This report provides analysis of the forecasting quality and describes the technical components and analysis used to provide the Army forecasts of recruiting difficulty.

Our Approach

The study team identified known and potential indicators of the conceptual factors believed to have a direct influence on desirable/adverse recruiting outcomes at the national level. In addition to publicly available information such as economic conditions and news stories, the research team identified Army data providing levels of accession missions, recruiting resources, and DEP levels; Army data allowing assessment of enlistment contract and DEP characteristics, such as recruit quality overall, DEP length, and whether waivers or bonuses were used; and recruiting-related information such as enlistment propensity, number of contracts written, and the number of recruiters available. RAND Arroyo Center then built a multiequation model that explicitly quantified the magnitude and lead time of the association between each of these indicators and desirable/adverse recruiting outcomes, such as success in meeting the contract mission, DEP length, and the training seat fill rate. The key to building this model was identifying economic, world event, and Army policy variables that predicted the recruiting environment with a sufficient lead time. In particular, the University of Michigan Consumer Sentiment (UMCSENT) Index, housing starts, and the 20- to 24-year-old male unemployment rate showed excellent predictive power over Army recruiting conditions 12 months into the future. Once we identified potential predictors, the study team "optimized" the model by selecting particular lag structures of the endogenous and exogenous variables to minimize the mean-squared forecast error. The resulting models were used to forecast the recruiting environment using coefficients from multivariate regression analysis of the associations of the selected indicators with each of the recruiting outcomes. The study team built both 12- and 24-month forecasts, where the 12-month forecast used 12 months of lagged variables, so that each month's forecast used real data from as recently as one year prior. The 24-month forecast estimated a separate model with 24 months of lagged variables used in the prediction. Since the 12-month forecast error was smaller, the 24-month forecast was only used for months 13 to 24.

Results of the forecasting model, together with the Recruiting Resource Model (RRM) (Knapp et al., 2018), were then used to develop strategies to determine the recruiting resource levels and mix among incentives, recruiters, and advertising and enlistment eligibility policies to address indications of changes in recruiting difficulty associated with improved/adverse recruiting outcomes. We provide an example of integrating the recruiting difficulty and recruiting resource models to formulate policy recommendations for identifying prospective changes in recruiting outcomes and taking related actions to address those changes. The illustrative recommendations discuss the lead time of indicators of prospective recruiting challenges or improvement in conjunction with the lead time needed for implementation and effective use of specific recruiting resources and eligibility policies to ensure cost-effective accomplishment of the accession requirement. Specifically, we demonstrate that, for an accession goal of 75,000, a worsening recruiting environment, represented by a 10-percentage-point decrease in U.S. Army Recruiting Command (USAREC) contract mission achievement for graduate alphas (GAs), leads to a $145 million increase in recruiting costs (assuming the efficient allocation of recruiting resources).

Organization of the Report

In Chapter Two, we review factors affecting recruiting difficulty and examine previous enlistment early warning systems. Chapter Three provides a discussion of our conceptual models, including the endogenous and exogenous factors leading to recruiting difficulty. We look at the seven-equation model, composed of three recruiting difficulty measures, and four endogenous recruiting resource measures. Chapter Four discusses data and measurement issues. Chapter Five discusses the process for optimizing the specification of the model (i.e., which variables are included, and how many lags). The goal is to minimize the mean-squared forecast error within the space of potential models. Chapter Six provides the forecasts using the optimized model. Chapter Seven gives recommendations for leveraging the forecasts from the recruiting difficulty index (RDI) model. Chapter Eight provides a short summary and conclusion.

CHAPTER TWO

Review of Factors Affecting Recruiting Difficulty

Enlistment Research from the Early Phases of the All-Volunteer Force

The literature on forecasting military enlistments dates back to at least the beginning of the all-volunteer force (AVF). Given the general uncertainty surrounding whether or not the AVF would be a success, economists were uncertain that economic incentives would be sufficient to induce young men to enlist in the armed forces (Ash, Udis, and McNown, 1983). Economic theory supposed that young adults face a choice between civilian and military employment and that there exists a military reservation wage that makes the potential recruit indifferent between the two. However, incorporated into the reservation wage is a compensating differential that reflects the individual's taste for the nonpecuniary aspects of military service. These tastes may lower the military reservation wage for those who have a strong taste for military service or may raise it for those who have weak preferences or aversion to military service. Importantly, these preferences may become more salient during times of war, when operational tempo is high or when geopolitical uncertainty increases.

During the initial phase of the all-volunteer force, forecasting models were primarily cross-sectional. This was driven by data limitations since, obviously, a long time series of data about the AVF was not available (see, for example, Walter Oi's study for the Gates Commission [Oi and Forst, 1971]). Later models not only focused on setting relative wages and evaluating the military/civilian pay ratio but also focused more attention on issues related to unemployment.

> Previous empirical studies of enlistment in the AVF have included the civilian unemployment rate as an additional explanatory variable. Until relatively recently the theoretical justification for doing so has not been obvious. . . . If the real wage in the civilian labor market does not instantaneously adjust downwards in response to excess supply, actual unemployment is likely to result, forcing job hunters into the recruitment office. It is assumed in the present study that individuals' perceptions of likely employment constraints in the civilian labor market are determined by the corresponding unemployment rate. (Ash, Udis, and McNown, 1983, p. 147)

However, Ash et al. (1983) find only limited evidence of unemployment rates' relationship with enlistments. They report finding lower pay elasticities than previous estimates and no statistically significant effect of unemployment on recruitment.[1]

Ash et al. (1983) are not the only researchers to find minimal effects of unemployment on recruitment. For example, Withers (1979) reports statistically significant effects of unemployment on recruiting, but the signs are opposite of what theory would predict (he finds that higher unemployment is associated with declining recruitment). This inverse relationship between unemployment and recruiting may occur if the services increase their selectivity during periods of high unemployment. Grissmer (1979) posits that increasing selectivity during periods of high unemployment means reducing the number of high school dropouts but maintaining desired recruitment levels through higher rates of unemployment-induced enlistments from the more select group. This could account for a weak or statistically insignificant unemployment effect observed for total volunteers. Commenting on Ash et al.'s (1983) work, Dale and Gilroy find large effects of both relative wages and unemployment on Army enlistment. They argue that contracts (rather than accessions) are the better metric for determining the supply of new recruits (Dale and Gilroy, 1985). Using monthly contracts data from the Defense Manpower Data Corporation (DMDC),

---

[1] They use a two-stage estimator for unemployment and do not discuss their first stage results, so it is difficult to discern if this is a consequence of the two-stage model's design.

Dale and Gilroy estimated a time-series model during only the post-draft AVF era—unlike Ash et al. (1983) who estimate a semiannual model using both draft and postdraft eras. Dale and Gilroy estimate an unemployment elasticity of 0.81 and 0.94 depending on the specification. Using the same specification, but focusing on Army accessions, there appears to be no relationship between unemployment and Army accessions. As we will discuss later, our model, like Dale and Gilroy (and for the reasons they suggest), uses recruiting difficulty measures based on contracts and controls for recruit quality.

Using quarterly data from across the United States, Brown (1985) finds that for the Army wage elasticities are 1.0 for high-quality recruits, and unemployment elasticities are about 0.5. That is, as unemployment increases by 1 percent, recruitment of high-quality candidates increases by about 0.5 percent. Additionally, Brown finds that Army recruiters increase the number of enlistees, but increases in other services' recruiters reduce the number of Army enlistees. Proportional increases in all service branch recruiters increase the number of Army enlistees. Advertising was not found to have a consistent effect.

Asch, Hosek, and Warner (2007) survey recruiting analyses covering before and after the end of the Cold War and the drawdown of the services in the early 1990s. These analyses began to take advantage of the more detailed administrative data that became available during this period in order to pursue more sophisticated methods. They compare high-quality Army contract elasticities for economic and recruiting resource variables across a variety of studies to include the unemployment rate (i.e., high-quality contracts corresponds to contracts written for enlistees that are high school graduates or seniors and that are in the top 50 percentiles of the Armed Forces Qualification Test (AFQT)—a standardized test meant to measure an individual's aptitude). Studies covering the periods both before and after the drawdown differ in the measurement of contract unemployment elasticity; however, all find that it is significant and plays an important role in the production of high-quality Army enlistment contracts. Estimates range from 0.15–0.16 after the drawdown (Murray and McDonald, 1999; Dertouzos and Garber, 2003) to 0.34 (Warner, Simon, and Payne, 2003). A more recent analysis of Army data from fiscal years 2000 to 2008 finds significant but small unemployment elasticities of 0.10—consistent with other past work (Asch et al., 2010). These analyses also find important relationships among recruiting resources—such as recruiters, advertising and enlistment incentives, and high-quality Army contracts.

Even from the earliest phases of recruiting research, researchers understood that the Army and other services had multiple policy levers that they manipulate depending on the recruiting environment. Some of these levers speak directly to the taste for military service mentioned earlier—including allowing persons who have a greater taste for service but who may be less educated, have a lower aptitude, need waivers, or have served previously but separated to join in greater numbers. Other options are designed to influence preference or to provide information (advertising), or to increase the ability of the Army to reach potential recruits (recruiters). Other options such as bonuses directly focus on the reservation wage component of military service. Finally, the choice of military occupation is a way to match recruit preferences to Army needs.

Forecasting Models: Goldberg Enlistment Early Warning System

Perhaps the best-known efforts to provide advanced warning about impending recruiting difficulty are the early efforts by Goldberg in 1982 and Goldberg et al. in 1984 and subsequent revisions in 2003 and 2015. Here we discuss the Goldberg and Kimko model from 2003 and its revision, Goldberg, Kimko, and Li (2015). In their 2003 paper, Goldberg and Kimko provide a comprehensive list of the items that affect Army recruiting. Among these include economic factors such as military/civilian pay, unemployment, Army education benefits, bonuses, recruiters, contract missions assigned to recruiters, Army advertising, and the size of the youth population.

Goldberg and Kimko estimate a model of the logarithm of total enlistments for high school graduate diploma holders and high school seniors separately for males and females using national, monthly data. They then build an enlistment forecast based on the forecasted unemployment rate. The early warning system models of this era use an externally produced forecast of the unemployment rate from the Blue Chip Economic Indicators. The initial model is estimated using monthly data from FY 1981 through CY 2000; this model underpredicted enlistments in the 1980s and overpredicted enlistments in the 1990s (Goldberg and Kimko, 2003, p. 31). Goldberg argues that there are a number of regime changes caused by policy shifts that occur almost every year. Goldberg and Kimko estimate the models separately by decade to examine these regime-change effects.

The 2003 version of the enlistment early warning models began to falter following the attacks on 9/11, the recession of 2002–2003, and the expansion of the Iraq war. The 2002–2003 recession allowed the Army to achieve its enlistment goals but, as casualties increased in Iraq, the Goldberg and Kimko model began to overpredict enlistments. The response was to revise the model and incorporate a new estimation strategy. First was the inclusion of war variables—including combat fatalities and operational tempo information such as the June 2007 to July 2008 Iraq surge. Second, Goldberg, Kimko, and Li (2015) revised the estimation strategy to include a switching regression that includes three equations: equation one is used when the recruiting goal is not achieved (a supply-limited regime), the second equation is used when the recruiting goal is met (a demand-limited regime), and the third equation estimates the probability of being in either regime—that is, a switch to determine which estimation equation should be used. All three equations are estimated simultaneously using maximum likelihood estimation. Unlike previous enlistment early warning systems, these models are estimated at the recruiting battalion level for each month and provide considerably more statistical power.

In all, the Goldberg models in their different incarnations provide the fundamental foundation for building future recruiting early warning systems. While the estimation strategies have changed, as have the number and types of independent predictors in the models, all of them use relative pay and unemployment as the primary factors that feed into the forecast. Goldberg and Kimko (2003) writes that "fluctuations in unemployment are the major cause of shifts in enlistment supply." Consequently, forecasting unemployment is extremely important for models that approach estimation in this way. However, comparisons of forecast errors for the Congressional Budget Office (CBO), Blue Chip Consensus, and the current administration estimates of gross domestic product (GDP) are typically larger during the peak of an expansion.[2] This is because turning points are especially difficult to predict. For example, the Iraqi invasion of Kuwait in 1990 led to a spike in oil prices, a shock to energy costs, and a subsequent decline in output as well as a decline in consumer confidence. These factors likely contributed to the ensuing recession but were extremely difficult to forecast. Similarly, it is likely that forecast errors in the unemployment rate will be larger at the peak of expansions, making early warning systems built on these types of estimation strategies likely to miss many of the turns. This is not a shortcoming of these models, but rather a reflection of the uncertainty of the regime shift.

---

[2] See U.S. Congress, Congressional Budget Office, *CBO's Economic Forecasting Record: 2017 Update*, Washington, DC: CBO, October 2017.

CHAPTER THREE

Conceptual Model

Many past analyses of recruiting have been single-equation models that analyzed the determinants of high-quality accessions. Some modelers were aware of the endogeneity of explanatory variables such as the number of recruiters and the use of enlistment bonuses, but there were few instances where an instrumental variable was used or, more generally, a system of equations was specified. Our model considers multiple outcomes of interest to the recruiting community, allows the outcomes to be interrelated in a multiequation model, includes exogenous variables based on theoretical considerations and past work, enables identification of the multiequation model, and permits lagged values of past outcomes to be included. Its purpose is accurate near-term forecasting of Army recruiting conditions—forecasts that can be used in selecting policy actions that respond cost-effectively to anticipated conditions.

In contrast, most prior models were oriented toward finding the causal effect of factors such as military/civilian pay, unemployment, and recruiting resources (recruiters, recruiting centers, bonuses, advertising) on high-quality enlistments. Other models were designed to reduce attrition or otherwise improve retention by examining factors that led to higher rates of first-term completion or reenlistment. In general, these models were intended to be structural models. Our predictive model sidesteps these cause-effect identification issues because causality is not required for a model to be an accurate predictor of near-term outcomes. Instead, lagged values of dependent variables can capture information about system dynamics and can be used in making near-term forecasts. Importantly, the objective of this model is to solve it in the space that minimizes the mean-squared forecast error (MSFE).

The main idea here is to start the model at a particular point in the solution space and find a local minimum (smallest forecast error). We continue specifying additional variables and lags of endogenous factors until we can no longer find a local minimum. Multiple starting points are used, although there is no systematic search algorithm designed to guarantee a global minimum.

Figure 3.1 introduces the conceptual model that captures the concept of recruiting difficulty. As past analyses suggest, recruiting difficulty is impacted by factors outside the Army's control (i.e., exogenous factors), such as global events and risk, social issues and views, and labor market and other economic conditions. In response, the Army has a variety of resources and eligibility policies that it can use to compensate for factors outside of its control. There are five steps to operationalizing the conceptual model:

1. Identify good measures of recruiting difficulty (outcomes)—these measures should correspond with experts' knowledge of the recruiting environment as well as objective measures of recruiting success.
2. Identify endogenous policy responses—once the Army recognizes a difficult recruiting environment, senior leaders can take multiple actions to overcome these difficulties, but different policy options have different costs and lead times.
3. Identify exogenous economic and environmental variables that can be used to forecast difficult (and easy) recruiting environments.
4. Estimate the model.
5. Forecast recruiting environment and validate pseudo-out-of-sample predictions against observed outcomes.

Because the Army responds to difficult recruiting environments by increasing recruiting resources and expanding recruit eligibility policies, a contemporaneous correlation may result between these resources or policies and recruiting outcomes. This contemporaneous correlation may lead to incorrect inferences regarding their effect on enlistment. For example, during difficult recruiting environments, the Army may choose to increase bonus amounts, in which case a contemporaneous correlation analysis would incorrectly infer that bonuses lead to lower

Figure 3.1
Conceptual Model of Recruiting Difficulty

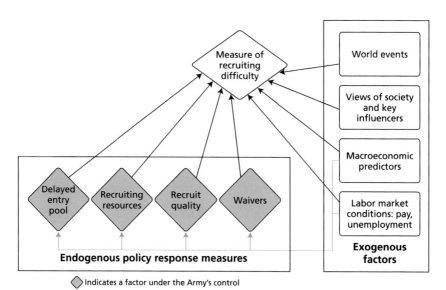

enlistment. A similar story may occur with the number of recruiters in the field and other policy options utilized by the Army.

Nonetheless, there is valuable information about the recruiting environment contained in the decision (both the timing and levels) to utilize these recruiting policies. To exploit this information, we separately model each of the main recruiting policy options with its own equation and then allow the lags of those policies to also predict recruiting difficulty measures.

Model Specification: Measures of Recruiting Difficulty (Outcomes)

CMMGA

We develop three measures of recruiting difficulty. Our first measure, CMMGA, is the most comprehensive. CMMGA stands for **c**ontracts **m**inus **m**ission (as a percentage of mission) for **g**raduate **a**lphas. GAs are defined as enlistees with a high school diploma who score at the fiftieth percentile or above on the AFQT. This direct measure of recruiting difficulty incorporates two important elements. First, it measures how many contracts are being written each month—this is a measure of labor supply and recruiter effectiveness. Second, it directly controls for recruit quality by focusing on GA recruits. This is a particularly important step given that the Army recruiting command has separate contract goals (missions) for GA, high school senior–alpha, and lower-quality recruits (those without a traditional high school diploma or equivalent credential or those who score below the fiftieth percentile on the AFQT). Focusing on GA contracts focuses on the largest and most supply-constrained portion of the Army's recruiting market and allows us to identify a poor recruiting environment even when overall contracts may meet goals through increased admittance of lower-quality recruits.

CMMGA is expressed as a percentage of the contract mission for GAs. That is, if the mission is for 5,000 GA contracts in a given month, and the Army only produces 4,000, then the CMMGA is $100 \times (4,000 - 5,000 / 5,000) = -20\%$. Positive numbers indicate contracts in excess of contract mission, while negative numbers indicate unmet contract goals.

CMMGA corresponds well with qualitative changes to the overall recruiting environment. Figure 3.2,[1] for example, shows that it tracks the deterioration of the recruiting environment that began in late 2003. CMMGA declined steadily throughout 2004 and 2005 before plateauing and remaining poor until early 2008. Similarly, improved recruiting conditions also corresponded to rises in CMMGA. As a result of the recession spanning December 2007 through June 2009 and the subsequent weak labor market recovery, the Army's recruiting environment improved dramatically. By early 2008, CMMGA had already started to reverse course, and by 2009 the Army was regularly exceeding its GA contract mission.

---

[1]   Both CMMGA and DEP length figures show the data used to build the model in black and subsequent data for out-of-sample validation in red. The Training Seat Fill Rate (TSFR) data were much noisier than these data series and are used for validation purposes.

Figure 3.2
CMMGA from FY 2003 to FY 2016

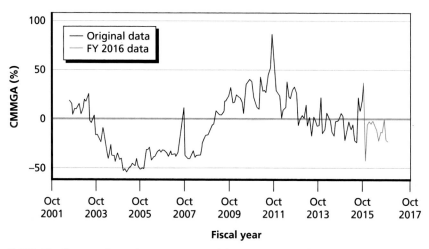

NOTE: The figure reflects the average monthly percentage difference between GA contract achievement versus mission (where 100-percent mission achievement is normalized to zero), starting from the first month of fiscal year 2003 (i.e., October 2002). The graph is based on the authors' calculations, using data from the USAREC missioning data base and the Regular Army (RA) Analyst file. It includes GA contracts and contract missions only. These values are calculated only for recruiting centers in the 50 U.S. states and Washington, D.C. "GA" refers to enlistees with at least a high school degree at the time of enlistment and who have scored in the top 50 percentiles on the AFQT. See the text for additional details.

There are a number of merits to CMMGA: it is scale free, and, by focusing on GAs, it controls for recruit quality. However, contracts and mission are both endogenous. Additionally, mission at time t might increase if mission was not met at time $t-1$, further compounding the endogeneity through an autocorrelated error structure. CMMGA provides a convenient way of summarizing the contract mission achievement outcomes, though an alternative would be separate equations for GA contracts and for mission, with appropriate lags of both variables in both equations. We do not pursue this option because a summary measure such as CMMGA provides the strongest signal to the Army about the recruiting environment—failing to achieve GA mission is a strong, clear message. Having separate equations for contracts and contract mission will not provide a univocal message.

As implied above, the CMMGA is not a measure of an accession shortfall. Rather, it is a measure that is sensitive to the difficulty in eliminating the possibility of such a shortage. In most years, the Army achieved its overall accession mission (i.e., an accession means the enlistee successfully ships out), yet declines in CMMGA suggest that it did so by filling out open training seats with lower-quality recruits. During our data period, only in FY 2005 did the Army miss its accession mission—regardless of quality—by 8 percent (Kapp, 2013). From FY 2003 through FY 2007, recruit quality also dropped dramatically (both in terms of the proportion who were high school graduates and AFQT scores). The Army reacted to the difficult recruiting environment by adding more than 2,500 recruiters to the existing recruiting force, spending more on advertising and bonuses, allowing older and more prior service candidates to enlist, relaxing some existing enlistment standards, and raising the number of waivers, especially conduct waivers. The Army also raised the maximum allowable enlistment bonus from $20,000 to $40,000 (Kapp, 2013, p. 4).

Delayed Entry Program Length

Once a recruit signs a contract, he or she is placed in the DEP before filling a training seat in Basic Combat Training (BCT). During periods when the recruiting environment is difficult, the average length of time waiting in the DEP declines. This is because during such periods recruiters have more training seat vacancies that need to be filled in the near term. As a consequence, contracts have nearer-term ship dates. In some cases, these ship dates may be within 30 days or less of signing the contract. When recruiting conditions are more favorable, the DEP fills with recruits whose presence is not immediately required to fill training seat vacancies. Consequently, contracted ship dates are scheduled further into the future. In exceptionally good recruiting periods, the *average* duration in DEP has reached 200 days. Average DEP lengths will vary during a year given the cyclical nature of training seats and accessions. For example, DEP lengths tend to be longer in October and November since BCT rarely begins in December. In general, "normal"

DEP lengths range from 90 to 150 days. DEP lengths shorter than 90 days reflect potential difficulty for USAREC in achieving the annual accession mission. Longer DEP lengths reflect better recruiting conditions, as noted, but are associated with more enlistees failing to follow through and ship for basic training.[2]

Figure 3.3 shows a similar boom-bust pattern in DEP length to that of CMMGA in Figure 3.2. In FY 2005, when the Army missed its overall accession mission, DEP length declined from 120 days in FY 2004 to a low of just over 30 days in August 2005. As the Great Reces-

Figure 3.3
DEP Length from FY 2003 to FY 2016

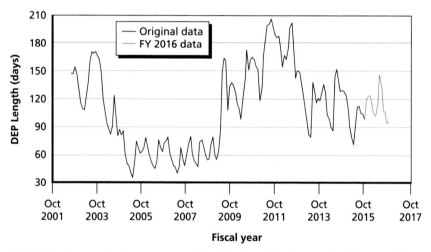

NOTE: The figure reflects average monthly DEP length in days starting from the first month of fiscal year 2003 (i.e., October 2002). The graph is based on the authors' calculations, using data from the RA Analyst file, which contains contract-level data regarding the length of time that an enlistee is projected to be in the DEP before shipping for basic training, by contracting month. See the text for additional details.

---

[2] Attrition can happen at the reception battalion before reporting to basic training. Basic training follows one of two standard paths for nonprior service (NPS) recruits depending on Military Occupational Specialty (MOS). The first path is BCT followed by Advanced Individual Training (AIT), which often involves transferring to a new station for the AIT. The second path is attending One Station Unit Training (OSUT), which combines BCT and AIT at one station.

sion set in, DEP length increased from 60 days to be consistently 100 or more days in a matter of months. Using CMMGA as a benchmark, DEP length appears to be an accurate indicator of recruiting difficulty with a slightly longer lag in its response to increased recruiting difficulty than the percentage of the GA contract mission achieved. We include DEP length as an additional indicator of recruiting difficulty. DEP length also contains information regarding non-GA recruits, making it useful as an additional outcome in our model.

Training Seat Fill Rate

Our final measure of recruiting difficulty is the TSFR (in percentage terms). Failing to fill training seats can create substantial costs for the Army in the form of unexploited economies of scale. Additionally, unfilled training seats can have implications for more advanced training and for unit shortfalls and readiness. The TSFR is considerably noisier than either CMMGA or DEP length and has an added disadvantage: it is the final step in the recruiting production process. Consequently, it is more likely to reflect a difficult recruiting environment after it has already arrived and may be indicative of severely difficult recruiting environments. Only after a period of shortened DEP lengths will TSFRs decline. Nevertheless, this measure helps us validate the other indicators of recruiting difficulty and incorporates a measure that most directly affects costs for the Army. It is also important for completeness. The Army has been slow to reprogram resources when there is evidence of recruiting difficulty. In our model, we have built three "canaries in coal mine." The first is CMMGA and will show recruiting difficulties within two to three months; as the trend lengthens, the situation becomes more clear. DEP length provides a slightly slower-to-respond secondary indicator. Concern should be raised when the two move in the same direction. Finally, once the Army has consistently failed to fill training seats, it has a full-blown difficult recruiting environment. Based on these three pieces of evidence, recruiting command should be able to alert senior leadership to the severity of the issue.

Figure 3.4 plots the time series of the TSFR from FY 2003 to FY 2016, the most notable points being the failed accession mission in FY 2005 where training seats were persistently missed. Improvement

Figure 3.4
TSFR from FY 2003 to FY 2016

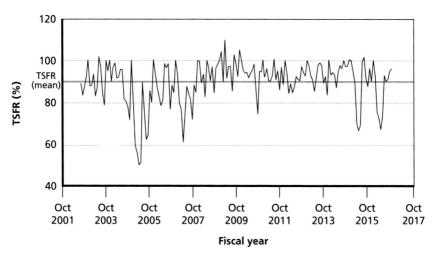

NOTE: The figure reflects the average monthly TSFR starting from the first month of fiscal year 2003 (i.e., October 2002). The graph is based on the authors' calculations, using data from the Army Training Requirements and Resources System (ATRRS). The TSFR reflects the fraction of the BCT and OSUT seats that are filled each month. The TSFR (mean) reflects the average training seat fill, which is around 90 percent.

starts in FY 2006. During the recession, the TSFR frequently reached or exceeded 100 percent. The historic average for the TSFR is approximately 90 percent.

Model Specification: Army Policy (Endogenous Responses)

As discussed in the conceptual model, there are a number of policy responses at the Army's disposal when faced with a difficult recruiting environment. One option is to reduce the "high-quality" targets for recruits, such as by allowing more general equivalency diploma (GED) holders to enter. However, the Department of Defense (DoD) has benchmarks in place, requiring that at least 90 percent of enlistees be high school graduates with diplomas or equivalent certifications.

Additionally, the DoD places limits on the proportion of recruits with AFQT scores below the national average who are allowed to enlist. Guidelines for the AFQT include that at least 60 percent of enlistees score above the national average (i.e., the fiftieth percentile), and only 4 percent at most can have test scores in the tenth to thirtieth percentiles. No enlistee who scores between the first and ninth percentiles can enlist. Consequently, the Army's ability to reduce the "high-quality" target is somewhat constrained. Furthermore, because CMMGA only counts contracts for graduate-alpha recruits, our CMMGA outcome measure will not account for changes in recruit quality.

There are a number of other policy responses that the Army can undertake when the recruiting environment is difficult, such as the period beginning in FY 2004 and ending in FY 2008. The Army reacted to the difficult recruiting environment through a variety of measures. These recruiting resources and recruit eligibility policies motivate the endogenous responses we include in our model and are detailed below.

Number of Recruiters on Duty

When the recruiting environment is difficult, the Army can respond by adding recruiters. Between FY 2003 and FY 2007, for example, the Army added 2,500 recruiters to its existing recruiting force. Discussions with USAREC indicate that it can take up to six months before new recruiters in the field are fully effective in recruiting. For the purposes of forecasting, the lag structure of this variable is therefore an important empirical question that we will address below.

Military Occupational Specialty Bonuses

Some occupations in the Army are more common (e.g., infantrymen, 11B) than others (e.g., cardiovascular specialist, 68N). In cases where a recruit is highly qualified and wants to serve in a hard-to-fill occupation, the Army will provide a monetary incentive for that soldier to agree to employment in that MOS. In the case of the cardiovascular specialist, for example, the MOS bonus available in March 2017 was $40,000 payable over a four-year enlistment term. In poor recruiting environments, the Army can increase the amounts payable or the number or enlistees eligible for such bonuses in order to meet its recruiting goals. In the FY 2003 through FY 2007 period, for example, the Army received the authority to increase the maximum allowable bonus from $20,000 to $40,000, where it currently stands.

Quick-Ship Bonuses

Rather than allow training seats to go vacant, the Army creates an incentive for enlistees to ship for BCT within 30 days. In March 2017, recruits who agreed to ship within 30 days were eligible for a $20,000 quick-ship (QS) bonus. Soldiers willing to ship from 31 to 60 days were eligible for an $8,000 bonus. As with MOS bonuses, the Army can increase the bonus amounts to incentivize an increase in enlistments.

Conduct Waivers

Potential recruits may fail to meet Army enlistment standards. Some of these persons can meet the criteria for medical, moral, administrative, or drug/alcohol waivers. Moral or "conduct" waivers deal with prior misconduct and apply to persons with multiple driving or non-driving offenses; the dominant subcategory involves serious nontraffic misdemeanors. Moral standards are designed to screen out recruits who are likely to become serious disciplinary problems. These disciplinary problems may divert resources from duties central to the Army, affect unit readiness, and affect the performance of Army missions. If a potential soldier has a history of repeated misdemeanors but has demonstrated that he has rehabilitated himself, then he can seek a conduct waiver and, following review and approval, be permitted to enlist. When recruiting conditions deteriorate, the Army can increase the number of conduct waivers it accepts, which it did between FY 2005 and FY 2009.

Model Specification: Exogenous Predictors

A bevy of literature on Army recruiting has found that relative military/civilian pay and the unemployment rate are important determinants of enlistment. Additionally, there are noneconomic factors that supplement and interact with these determinants. Increased probability of combat, for example, may both deter risk averse recruits from enlisting and increase the Army's demand for recruits. Consequently, we include measures of risk spanning from Army casualty rates to an index of global geopolitical uncertainty. Below, we describe the full set of exogenous predictors that we include in the model.

Economic Variables

Our final model includes three economic indicators: (1) the national unemployment rate for 20- to 24-year-old males, (2) national housing starts, and (3) the UMCSENT Index. Rather than include these measures independently, we first estimate a principal components factor model and extract the first principal component. This allows us to utilize the common variance of the economic indicators to predict CMMGA, DEP length, and the TSFR.

The results from the principal component analysis (PCA) are shown below in Table 3.1. The number of observations is 203. We note that the PCA results have one eigenvalue greater than 1.0, indicating that the economic variables load on a single factor. We also note that the unemployment rate loads negatively, while the consumer sentiment and housing starts load positively. This is in keeping with the principal factor being an overall measure of the strength of the economy. In Table 3.2, the factor loadings are nearly identical in magnitude, suggesting that each variable contributes approximately equally to the composite economic measure. We discuss our search for economic variables in more detail in Chapter Four.

Table 3.1
Principal Component Analysis: Economic Variables—Eigenvalues

Component	Eigenvalue	Difference	Proportion	Cumulative
Comp1	2.4471	2.1121	0.8157	0.8157
Comp2	0.3350	0.1170	0.1117	0.9273
Comp3	0.2180		0.0727	1.0000

Table 3.2
Principal Component Analysis: Economic Variables—Factor Loadings

Variable	Comp1	Comp2	Comp3
Unemployment rate for 20- to 24-year-old males	−0.5897	0.2430	0.7702
UMCSENT Index	0.5627	0.8078	0.1759
Housing starts	0.5794	−0.5371	0.6131

Adverse Events

Most previous models of enlistment have focused nearly exclusive attention on the economic factors that lead to changes in enlistments. The model presented in this paper adds a series of measures that are likely to change youths' perceived risk of joining the Army or to alter parents' or other influencers' perceptions of risks. This includes an index of adverse events captured by a systematic search of LexisNexis, hostile death and casualty rates, and a geopolitical risk measure. These adverse events measures can also reflect recruiting demand, as the Army may increase its recruiting targets in times of higher geopolitical risk and war.

As in the case of the economic variables, we combine the results of five keyword searches of adverse events from the LexisNexis database using principal component analysis. The searches relate to deployments, deaths, conflicts, health, and assaults on service members. As shown in Table 3.3, the PCA yields one eigenvalue greater than 1.0, and, as shown in Table 3.4, all the measures load positively on the latent component. For the second eigenvalue, the factor loadings have two elements (health and assaults) that are reversed in sign, making that factor difficult to interpret.[3] Additionally, a confirmatory factor analysis supports a single eigenvalue and a single latent structure.

---

[3] It is possible that deployments and deaths are perceived to be deployment-related risks, while health and assault issues may be perceived as general conditions of serving in the Army.

Table 3.3
Principal Component Analysis: Adverse Events—Eigenvalues

Component	Eigenvalue	Difference	Proportion	Cumulative
Comp1	2.4226	1.4317	0.4845	0.4845
Comp2	0.9909	0.3165	0.1982	0.6827
Comp3	0.6744	0.1010	0.1349	0.8176
Comp4	0.5734	0.2346	0.1147	0.9323
Comp5	0.3387		0.0677	1.0000

Table 3.4
Principal Component Analysis: Adverse Events—Factor Loadings

Variable	Comp1	Comp2	Comp3	Comp4	Comp5
Deployments	0.4127	0.4311	−0.5961	0.5300	−0.0873
Deaths	0.3911	0.4648	0.7581	0.1928	0.1381
Health	0.5100	−0.4162	0.1344	−0.0294	−0.7401
Assaults	0.4476	−0.5982	−0.0316	0.2065	0.6310
Conflicts	0.4651	0.2588	−0.2255	−0.7990	0.1657

Finally, we utilize an index of geopolitical risk (Caldara and Iacoviello, 2018) that uses news stories containing terms related to geopolitical tensions as its basis. This index is monthly and runs from 1985 to the present. The geopolitical risk index has proven to be a good proxy measure for geopolitical risk. Caldara and Iacoviello find a positive association between their measure and lower oil prices as well as higher corporate credit spreads. In emerging economies, they find that a higher geopolitical risk index is predictive of lower economic activity, with the relationship stronger in higher-risk countries.

Bathtub and Other Time Controls
In recruiting, the months of February, March, and April correspond to particularly difficult months to fill training seats. Recently graduated high school seniors typically fill summer month training seats,

and the additional contracts signed in these months fill autumn training seats. The gap created by BCT not starting in December means that there are more January seats to fill, typically by contracts written in the autumn. From February to April, high school graduates recruited in the winter months primarily fill training seats intended for high-quality recruits. Since high school graduates available for work in winter months represent a narrower labor market from which to draw for enlistments, it makes seats in February to April more difficult to fill. This recurring pattern has led to these months being nicknamed the "bathtub" months, reflecting the natural dip in accessions during these months. We create a measure known as the "bathtub" measure, which reflects the average expected fill rate for these training seats as of three months prior, based on the size of the DEP at that time.[4] For example, in good recruiting conditions, the fill rate for April training seats based on the number of DEP participants in January may approach 100 percent.[5] In difficult recruiting conditions, this number is typically below 15 percent (in FY 2005–FY 2007, it averaged 10 percent). We incorporate this bathtub measure—reflecting the average fill rate three months prior to February, March, and April of the preceding fiscal year—as an exogenous measure capturing persistently difficult recruiting conditions.

In addition to the bathtub measure, we also include a series of month dummy variables and a linear time trend. Not every equation includes the bathtub, month, and year variables. We provide the actual specifications for each equation in Tables A.1 and A.2 of Appendix A.

---

[4] As mentioned earlier, we consider three months (90 days) to be the lower bound for USAREC to ensure it will achieve the annual accession mission.

[5] In calculating the fill rate for future months, we use the G-1 mission letter that is current as of the start of that month. For example, if in January, the accession mission for April is 5,000, then 5,000 is used as the denominator in January's April TSFR calculation. This is true even if the mission for April is changed during or after January. If, for example, the accession mission for April is lowered to 4,000 during January, then the denominator in February's April fill-rate calculation would be lowered to 4,000, but January's April TSFR calculation would remain the same. This calculation reflects the information available at the start of each month regarding future fill rates. See Appendix C for more details.

CHAPTER FOUR

Data

Data were collected from a number of sources, broadly divided into three categories: military data, nonmilitary national data aggregated by the St. Louis Federal Reserve Bank, and nonmilitary national data capturing measures related to the military. In this chapter, we review these data sources and how they are linked to create the measures referenced in Chapter Three. We conclude this chapter with some more technical notes about the timing of when measures were calculated and how occasional missing data were imputed. The end result of the data collection is a national-level analytical data set with monthly measures covering August 2002 until September 2016. In the appendix, we provide a user guide for updating this analytical data set so that the Army can update the model. A detailed discussion of the data, its sources, and our manipulation of the measures is provided in Appendix C.

Military Data

Army data are drawn primarily from databases maintained by the U.S. Army Human Resources Command (HRC), USAREC, and U.S. Training and Doctrine Command (TRADOC), as well as from strategic guidance issued by the Office of the Deputy Chief of Staff, G-1, U.S. Army.

National Economic and Demographic Data

The St. Louis Federal Reserve Bank maintains a collection of over 384,000 U.S. and international economic and demographic time series. From this database, we collect information on the overall and male age 20–24 unemployment rates (U.S. Bureau of Labor Statistics, 2017a, 2017c); crude oil prices (U.S. Energy Information Administration, 2017a); new private housing starts (U.S. Census Bureau, 2017); U.S. consumer sentiment index (University of Michigan, 2017a); leading index for the United States (Federal Reserve Bank of St. Louis, 2017); median civilian nominal earnings for age 16–24 working males (U.S. Bureau of Labor Statistics, 2017b); and emergency unemployment compensation transfers to individuals (U.S. Bureau of Economic Analysis, 2017).[1]

National Military-Related Measures

Past work has theorized that attitudes and perceptions may influence the willingness to enlist. Attitudes can be influenced by perceptions or observations of risk. We collected a number of measures meant to capture the unobserved notion of risk that might negatively influence enlistments, including measures of adverse events in the news, military-related deaths, and a geopolitical risk measure. We include measures of adverse events in the news that are based on historical keyword searches from an archive of Associated Press (AP) news stories through September 2013, and then LexisNexis searches of those key works after September 2013.

Counts of military-related deaths are collected from the iCasualties database, which tracks service related deaths and whether or not the cause of death was related to a hostile action (e.g., hostile fire). We considered measures of total and hostile deaths as part of the analysis.

---

[1]   These series can be found at the Federal Reserve Economic Data (FRED) website fred .stlouisfed.org. The series codes are LEU0252886300A (wages) and B1590C1A027NBEA (EUC).

Finally, Caldara and Iacoviello (2018) construct a measure of geopolitical risk by counting the number of articles mentioning phrases related to geopolitical tensions in 11 international newspapers. This methodology takes a broader approach than our adverse events measure by focusing more on broad risks, tensions, and threats.

CHAPTER FIVE

Optimizing the Forecast Model

In this chapter, we discuss how previous forecasting models of enlistment have been implemented. We then turn our attention to developing the intuition behind our multiequation endogenous regressor model. The specific implementation of this model requires (1) variable selection, (2) functional form transformation of each measure, (3) a strategy for determining which measures improve the quality of prediction, and (4) the results of that optimization process. We discuss each of these steps of model development below.

Most forecasting models of enlistments (see in particular, Goldberg and Kimko, 2003; Goldberg et al., 2015) rely on forecasting the main exogenous predictors of enlistment and then using the forecasted predictors to forecast enlistment. In the case of Goldberg and Kimko (2003), the exogenous determinants of enlistment are the relative pay of military enlistees and civilians and the unemployment rate. Recent revisions to the original Goldberg model include the addition of a series of war variables, including military fatalities in Iraq and Afghanistan and dummy indicators for operational tempo (surges) (Goldberg et al., 2015). This strategy may be problematic two reasons. First, the relative ratio of military pay was significantly increased in 2000 (Hosek and Sharp, 2001; Asch, 2003) as a result of the National Defense Authorization Act, which made military pay much more competitive with civilian pay. Forecasting these types of exogenous shocks is difficult, and ultimately leads to problematic forecasts of enlistments. And, annual pay increases (typically in January) do not provide enough within-year variation to identify recruiting difficulty. That is, each pay increase takes place at a single point in a year; consequently, it is not surprising that this annual variation was insufficient to predict monthly recruiting difficulty.[1] Additionally, bonus pay and special incentive pay can comprise a significant portion of compensation, which is why we model these variables simultaneously. As a result, the ratio of regular military to civilian pay is not an important determinant of enlistment in our models. The second problem with using forecasted predictors is that each exogenous determinant of enlistment must be forecasted before the enlistment forecast can be estimated. This limits the number of exogenous predictors that an analyst can use to those that can be adequately modeled and forecasted.

Instead of relying on forecasts of the exogenous factors, we look for variables that are leading indicators of enlistment (and by proxy, its exogenous contemporaneous predictors) and use these indicators in our forecasting model. That is, we search for variables that have predictive power 12- to 24-months in advance of recruiting outcomes and use them to forecast these outcomes 24 months into the future.

For example, Figure 5.1 below plots the 12-month lagged UMCSENT Index (reverse scaled—the y-axis goes from 100 to 50 instead of 50 to 100) against CMMGA. The 12-month lag demonstrates the 12-month predictive potential of the UMCSENT Index by aligning the current month observation for CMMGA with the UMCSENT Index measure from 12 months ago. First, we note that the correlation between CMMGA and the index is negative—as recruiting difficulty worsens (CMMGA declines), consumer sentiment is generally improving. This suggests that recruiting difficulty is at least partially driven by the economic opportunities of the private sector. The contemporaneous correlation between CMMGA and consumer sentiment is −0.47.

---

[1]   Another reason for the lack of predictive power for basic pay or regular military compensation is that much of the increase in relative pay was due to the stagnation of young civilian workers' wages—which occurred very slowly over the decade. The indexation of military pay to the employment cost index raised military pay relative to civilian pay, but this growth has disproportionately come from increases in the basic allowance housing (BAH) (Hosek, Asch, and Mattock, 2012). It is unlikely that BAH influenced first-term soldiers to enlist since first-term soldiers are more likely to be single and have lower BAH and are least likely to live off base/post.

Figure 5.1
CMMGA and UMCSENT Index (Consumer Sentiment Reverse Scaled and Lagged 12 Months)

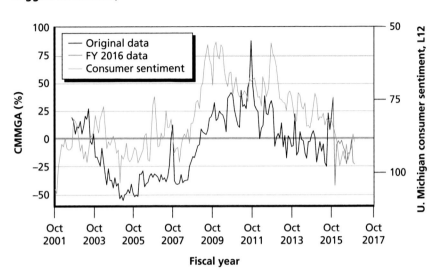

NOTE: The graph is based on the authors' calculations of CMMGA ((contracts − contract mission) / contract mission for GAs) using data from the USAREC missioning database, RA Analyst file, and the UMCSENT Index. See text for additional details.

However, the correlation increases as we correlate contemporaneous CMMGA with lags of consumer sentiment. A four-month lag generates a correlation of −0.52; an eight-month lag generates a correlation of −0.58; and the correlation peaks with a 12-month lag at −0.66. The correlation stays above −0.60 through 20 months. This provides suggestive evidence that the current CMMGA measures can be estimated using consumer sentiment measures from 12 months ago. Once we estimate the model coefficients we can then run the data forward month by month to calculate forecasts. If the current month is denoted as t, we can use the index from $t - 12$ to estimate the model. Then, we use the $t - 11$ consumer sentiment to generate the one-month-ahead forecast for $CMMGA_{t+1}$ and the current month of consumer sentiment to generate the 12-month forecast for $CMMGA_{t+12}$.

In our final model, all the exogenous variables enter the model with a 12-month lag. These exogenous variables include the economic factors discussed previously (unemployment rate for 20- to 24-year old males, housing starts, UMCSENT Index); the adverse events variables from LexisNexis (deployments, deaths, health, assaults, and conflicts); total and hostile U.S. military deaths; and the geopolitical risk index.

Variable Selection: Starting Point

We started with a long list of exogenous variables that could potentially affect the supply of and demand for high-quality recruits. The set of candidate variables include those variables from surveys of civilian attitudes about the Army (influencer likely to recommend enlistment, influencer likely to support enlistment, influencer likely to oppose enlistment, youth positive or negative views of Army); the adverse events variables; the geopolitical risk measure from Caldara and Iacoviello (2018); total and hostile U.S. military deaths; and the ratio of civilian weekly wages to military pay. As mentioned in Chapter Three, we considered a wide variable of macroeconomic and demographic indicators. We tested measures such as youth obesity rates, incarceration rates, high school graduation rates, college attendance rates, and a broad range of other economic factors (multiple measures of unemployment and labor underutilization; leading indicators such as oil prices, stock market indices, and leading indicator indices). Variables were included as candidates for optimization if they either proved a statistically significant predictor at the 5 percent level in the CMMGA or DEP length equations or reduced the $CV_{h=12}$ criteria (discussed below) when included in all seven equations. The result was that the macroeconomic index, adverse events, total and hostile U.S. military deaths, and geopolitical risk variables became candidates for inclusion in each equation of the final model, and, as we discuss later, were ultimately kept in the final model.

In terms of endogenous lag structure, we started from the assumption that each equation only required one lag in its own variable, then proceeded to search for additional required lagged endogenous variables in the manner described below.

Functional Form

Estimates from regression equations are strongly influenced by the choice of variables included in the model and the lag structure; however, the functional form of each variable in the model can also influence the model's parameter estimates. For example, choosing to include a factor variable that combines economic regressors (as opposed to including each economic regressor individually) may have large effects on model fit and the quality of the forecast. Throughout the model-building phase we tested a number of alternate functional forms for each regressor. In what follows we discuss a series of technical decisions that influenced model fit and interpretation. We begin by discussing transformations of the most important variables in the model—CMMGA and DEP length—which are the primary outcomes of the model. We then discuss the transformations for endogenous regressors. In general, most of the regressors were converted to rates such as recruiters per contract (the inverse of contracts per recruiter) or MOS or QS bonus rate per contract. This transformation is helpful because measuring variables in this way ensures that our measures are predictors of poor (or good) recruiting conditions rather than a simple increase (or decline) in overall contracts written.

First, we standardized CMMGA and DEP length because our optimization procedure requires a measure for each outcome that is scale invariant. We create the following transformed version of each variable in period $t = 1$ to $t = T$:

$$y_t = \frac{\left(y_t^{Trimmed} - \left(\frac{1}{T}\right)\sum_{t=1}^{T} y_t^{Trimmed} \right)}{\text{st. dev.}\left(y_t^{Trimmed} \right)},$$

where

$$y_t^{Trimmed} = \left(y_t^{unstandardized} - m_y \times \min_{t \in (1,T)} \{ y_t \} \right)^{\frac{1}{2}},$$

and $m_{CMMGA} = 1.25$, $m_{DEP\ length} = 0.75$. Here $m_y \times \min_{t \in (1,T)} \{ y_t \}$ serves as the lower bound on each of our key outcome variables and $\bar{y}_t^{Trimmed}$ is the mean of the trimmed series. This set of restrictions does not allow our forecasts to reach lower than 1.25 times the lowest observed value of CMMGA. Similarly, it does not allow our forecasts to reach lower than 0.75 times the lowest observed value of average monthly DEP length. Taking the square root of the expression on the right-hand side of y_t^{Trimmed} allows our forecasts to approach these lower bounds smoothly, and subtracting by the lower bound ensures that all outcome values are positive and relative to a common minimum.

Second, the other endogenous variables that are transformed include conduct waivers, MOS bonuses, QS bonuses, and recruiters on duty. Numbers of conduct waivers, MOS bonuses, and QS bonuses are divided by total contracts written, turning them into proportions. This ensures that these variables reflect changes in recruit composition necessitated by poor recruiting conditions rather than a simple increase in overall contracts written. Recruiters on duty are included in the model as the inverse of recruiters on duty divided by total enlistment mission. Thus, it measures the average contract mission for each recruiter. This measure should go down when the Army responds to poor recruiting conditions by increasing the number of assigned recruiters.

The training seat endogenous variable is not usable for the month of December because very few training seats exist between Thanksgiving and Christmas. As a consequence, we construct a cubic spline to interpolate the zero in December.

Many of the exogenous variables in the model necessitate pre-model transformations as well. Casualties and hostile deaths are turned into rates by dividing by total recruiting contracts written. As mentioned in Chapter Three, the UMCSENT Index, the 20- to 24-year-old male unemployment rate, and national housing starts are combined into a principal component for inclusion. Similarly, the five adverse event measures are combined into a single principal component. Before conducting the principal component analysis, a transformation was required due to a change in the data collection. Beginning with September 2013, the sources for the adverse event measure changed from an archive of AP news articles to a LexisNexis search query of AP news articles. This created a substantial, one-time change in the magnitude of articles containing each keyword. In order to unify this measure, we used the following, simple procedure for each keyword. First, we ran the following regression:

$$count_t^k = \alpha_1^k + \alpha_2^k \, \| \, \{month \geq September\, 2013\} + u_t^k,$$

$$k = \begin{cases} \text{deployments, injuries and deaths, medical support} \\ \text{and well-being, military crime and improprieties,} \\ \text{and mentions of Middle Eastern conflicts} \end{cases}.$$

Then, for a given k, the series we use for the principal component analysis is $\hat{\alpha}_1^k + \hat{u}_t^k$.

Criteria for Optimization

Given the prohibitively large set of potential combinations, we employed a systematic method for determining which of our candidate exogenous variables and lagged endogenous variables to include in each model equation. Simply including "everything" in the model is likely to lead to model overfitting and erroneous forecasts due to high variance. Additionally, given that many of the variables measure similar concepts, overfitting introduces multicollinearity that eliminates meaningful predictor covariance. This is why, for example, we combined all the economic variables in a single factor and extracted the common variance using principal component analysis.

Pseudo-out-of-Sample Predicted Mean-Squared Forecast Error

A simple rule for determining whether a forecast model is improving when additional regressors are added is to compare the rolling MSFE for two different specifications. Calculating the forecast error requires *both* making a forecast and realizing the true outcome. That is, we can denote our seven-equation model that aims to forecast outcomes in time t at time $t - 12$:

$$y_t = \beta X_{t-12} + \rho_1 y_{t-1} + \rho_2 y_{t-2} + \rho_3 y_{t-3} + e_t,$$

where y_t is a 7×1 vector of our endogenous variables, X_{t-12} is a $k \times 1$ vector of exogenous predictors (of which there are k), and $y_{t-\ell}$ is the vector of endogenous variables in s lags. β is a matrix of $7 \times k$ parameters to be estimated on the exogenous variables and ρ_ℓ is a matrix of 7×7 parameters to be estimated. In general, the forecast error is defined (where the accents denote estimated quantities) as:

$$ y_t - \hat{\beta} X_{t-12} + \hat{\rho}_1 \hat{y}_{t-1} + \hat{\rho}_2 \hat{y}_{t-2} + \hat{\rho}_3 \hat{y}_{t-3} \equiv \hat{e}_t. $$

Note that here, the lagged endogenous outcomes have to be estimated using the simultaneous equation model as well. Only X_{t-12} is known at the time of the forecast (12 months out, or $t-12$). The ideal forecast model minimizes $\mathbb{E}[\hat{e}_t^2]$, the mean-squared forecast error. However, since y_t is unknown at the time of the forecast, $\hat{e}_t^2$ is a theoretical object.

One way around this is to compute the "pseudo-out-of-sample" predicted mean forecast error (SOOS PMFE). To calculate this measure, researchers first need to set aside enough observations to estimate the model from the beginning of a time series—for example, 2002 through 2009 in our sample. In the next step, the forecast is projected forward and compared to the true value in the data—in the same example, the forecast value for 2011m1 (12 months ahead) with the true value for 2011m1. This process is then repeated by adding one additional observation to the data in each subsequent step. Continuing with the example, this involves estimating the model 72 times and making 72 forecasts and recovering the squared errors in each case.

This strategy has intuitive appeal and attractive time-series properties. Unlike the well-known Akaike Information Criterion (AIC) and Schwarz Information Criterion (SIC), the SOOS PMFE can be generalized beyond one-step-ahead forecasts to longer horizons. Multistep forecasts have overlapping dependence, which means "that the correct penalty does not simplify to a scale of the number of parameters" as in the case of the one-step-ahead forecast (Hansen, 2010). Consequently, the AIC and SIC are not correctly calculated in these multistep forecasts. Furthermore, fitting models using the strategy of minimizing the SOOS PMFE is equivalent to maximum likelihood estimation of a stationary time series, which results in efficient parameter estimation for correctly specified time series models with normally distributed errors (McElroy and Wildi, 2013).

However, a significant downside to using the SOOS PMFE criterion is that it is heavily reliant on the behavior of the time series during the period that is set aside. Each of the 72 estimations alluded to above would include this initial period, meaning that the forecasts are tilted toward reflecting the behavior of CMMGA or DEP length in the 2002 through 2009 period. Thus, while we present results from the SOOS PMFE exercise in Chapter Six, we will rely on a selection criterion more suited for our setting, described below.

Cross Validation Leave-h-Out

Hansen (2010) suggests an alternative cross-validation (CV) method that circumvents these issues. The goal is to minimize the residual from the regression where we "leave out" observations in the middle of the time series, then forecast the left-out observations. We select a model specification that minimizes the mean of the squared residuals from all of these regressions where the leave-out window systematically moves for each estimation. The following figures provide an example of a $CV_{h=12}$ (leave-12-out cross validation). Figure 5.2 starts by simply plotting the data for CMMGA over time, from 2003 through 2015.

In Figure 5.3 we have removed 23 periods from the $(2h-1)$ where h is the estimation window of 12 months. We remove the second 12-month period so that the immediately adjacent months can have no influence on the forecast.

We then estimate the model using all the remaining data and calculate a forecast for the twelfth month of missing data in the leave-out window (Figure 5.4). Using the actual data and the forecast, we calculate the MSFE for the forecast window. This is shown in Figure 5.5 as the squared area between the blue line and the black dashed line.

We do this exercise for the CMMGA and DEP length equations for each time period from August 2002 to the end of the data in September 2015 and for each model specification (i.e., each combination of candidate predictor variables for a given equation). Consequently,

Figure 5.2
CV in Practice: CMMGA

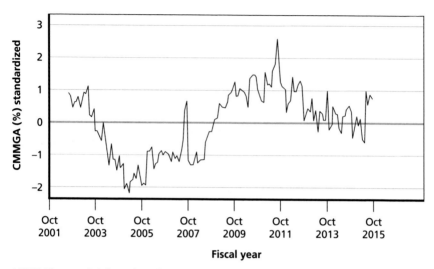

NOTE: The graph is based on the authors' calculations of CMMGAs using data from the USAREC missioning database and the RA Analyst file.

Figure 5.3
CV in Practice: Leave Out 2*(12) – 1

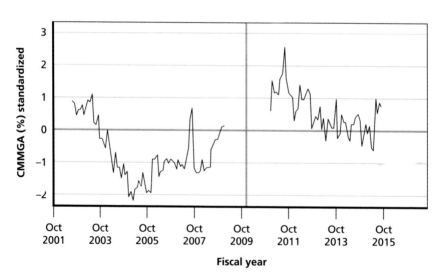

NOTE: This is the first figure in a sequence of three figures meant to illustrate the process for optimizing the forecast model.

Figure 5.4
CV in Practice: Forecast 12

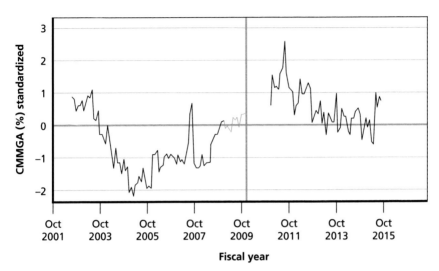

NOTE: This is the second figure in a sequence of three figures meant to illustrate the process for optimizing the forecast model.

Figure 5.5
CV in Practice: Comparing Forecast to Actual

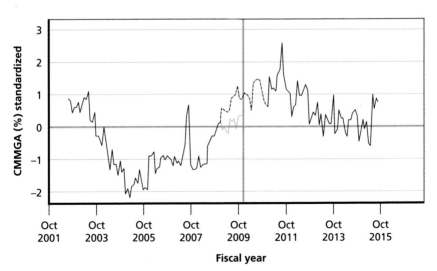

NOTE: This is the third figure in a sequence of three figures meant to illustrate the process for optimizing the forecast model.

we estimate residuals 136 times[2] each for CMMGA and DEP length within each specification. The mechanics of the model can be summarized as follows. Letting $s \in [2002m8, 2015m9]$, define

$$\tilde{e}_s \equiv y_s - \tilde{\beta}X_{s-12} + \tilde{\rho}_1\tilde{y}_{s-1} + \tilde{\rho}_2\tilde{y}_{s-2} + \tilde{\rho}_3\tilde{y}_{s-3},$$

where the matrices of parameters are estimated by fitting ordinary least squares models for all seven equations *excluding observations* $\{s - 11,\ldots, s,\ldots,s + 11\}$. Then, for a given model (i.e., a given set of potential predictor variables),

$$CV_{h=12}^y = \frac{1}{T} \sum_{s=2002m8}^{2015m9} \tilde{e}_s^2,$$

where T is the length of the time series from $2002m8$ to $2015m9$. Hansen (2010) shows that CV_h converges in probability to the mean forecast error for an h-step ahead forecast. Thus, under certain regularity assumptions, the minimum of the CV_h will also converge to the minimum of the MSFE—the ideal forecast model. Since we have two outcome variables of interest—CMMGA and DEP length—we choose the set of predictor variables in each equation that generates the lowest estimated $0.5 \times CV_{h=12}^{CMMGA} + 0.5 \times CV_{t=12}^{DEP\,length}$. This places an equal weight on optimizing the forecasts of each variable. We use the TSFR as an external validity check and do not optimize over that outcome.

Optimization Process

Choosing the set of exogenous variables and lag structure of the endogenous variables in each of the seven simultaneous equations involves

---

[2]   The total period of the model excludes the first 11 months since we can only make the first 12-month forecast after 11 months have elapsed. For the same reason, the last 11 months are also not used in the final model estimates. August 2002 through September 2015 is 158 months (13 years, 2 months); constructing the forecast in the twenty-third month yields 136 months.

a similar trade-off between lowering bias by including an increased number of lags and lowering variance by limiting the number of lag terms in each equation. In order to choose the correct endogenous variable lag structure in each of the seven equations, we also employed the CV_{12} criterion. However, due to the intractable number of combinations of endogenous and exogenous variables across the seven equations in the model, we had to take a systematic approach to limiting the search space. We optimize the forecasting model in three main phases:

1. Choose a set of exogenous variables to start each equation. These variables were chosen using a combination of economic theory and previous research. We then optimize the inclusion of lagged endogenous variables in each equation of the model, one at a time, until the set of variables in each equation does not change using the CV leave-12-out technique discussed earlier. Our optimization search stopped with three lags of any endogenous variable. We found that fourth and fifth lags were not producing meaningful improvements in fit. In general, each phase of the process resulted in significant improvements in model fit.

2. Holding the lagged endogenous variable structure fixed, we optimized the inclusion of 12-month-lagged exogenous variables in each equation of the model, one at a time, until the MSFE does not change. Throughout this phase we tested many variables that were not included in the final model.

3. Holding the newly optimized set of exogenous variables fixed, we reoptimize the endogenous lag structure in the same way as Phase I.

In Table 5.1 we summarize the improvement in the MSFE across the three stages of model optimization.

We also took three additional measures between Phases I and II that are of note. First, the initial model was a five-equation model that did not include recruiters on duty and TSFR as a percentage of the target as endogenous variables. These were added as a result of feedback from a briefing with USAREC and G-1. Second, as discussed above, we combined some similar variables into principal components in order

Table 5.1
MSFE at Each Stage of Model Fit

	Phase I	Phase II	Phase III
Optimize exogenous variables	Start value: 55.94	21.77 (56% improvement)	
Optimize endogenous variables	49.76 (11% improvement)		19.34 (11% improvement)

to reduce prediction error. One factor analysis combined adverse events from deployment, deaths, health, assaults, and conflicts into an adverse events principal component. The other factor analysis combined the UMCSENT Index, housing starts, and the civilian unemployment rate for 20- to 24-year-old men into a macroeconomic principal component. Finally, we included the geopolitical risk measure.

Overall, the result of the Phase I optimization was to lower the MSFE from 55.94 at the outset to 49.76 at the end of optimizing the lagged endogenous regressors. This represents an 11 percent reduction in MSFE using the CV_{12} criteria. In Phase II we made a number of changes to the model (see Tables 5.2, 5.3, and 5.4 for a summary of changes), added new regressors, and dropped some poorly performing regressors. The changes in MSFE using the CV_{12} criteria were much more impressive than for optimizing over the lagged endogenous regressors. In Phase II the MSFE declined from 49.76 to 21.77— slightly more than 56 percent.

After Phase III of the optimization the MSFE using the CV_{12} criteria fell 21.77 to 19.34, resulting in another 11 percent decline. Once the optimization had been completed, the overall model fit was very high. Across all equations the R-squared averaged 0.8736, with the worst-performing equation being TSFR (R-squared = 0.6231). In Table 5.5 we provide root mean-squared error (RMSE) and R-squared for each equation.

Table 5.2
Implementation of CV: Phase I

Exogenous Variables	Endogenous Variables
Fixed in this step:	**Optimized in this step. Result:**
CMMGA equation:	CMMGA equation:
Relative average civilian to military pay for	1 lag in CMMGA
16- to 24-year-olds	1 lag in DEP length
UMCSENT Index	1 lag in conduct waivers
Civilian unemployment rate	1 lag in QS bonuses
Crude oil prices	2 lags in MOS bonuses
Month fixed effects	DEP length equation:
Calendar year trend	2 lags in CMMGA
DEP length equation:	2 lags in DEP length
UMCSENT Index	1 lag in conduct waivers
Civilian unemployment rate	2 lags in QS bonuses
Crude oil prices	1 lag in MOS bonuses
Emergency unemployment insurance	Conduct waivers equation:
Bathtub months difficulty measure	1 lag in CMMGA
Month fixed effects	1 lag in DEP length
Calendar year trend	1 lag in conduct waivers
Conduct waivers equation:	QS bonuses equation:
UMCSENT Index	2 lags in CMMGA
Civilian unemployment rate	1 lag in DEP length
Crude oil prices	2 lags in conduct waivers
Housing starts	2 lags in QS bonuses
U.S. leading indicator index	MOS bonuses equation:
Recruiters on duty	2 lags in CMMGA
Bathtub months difficulty measure	2 lags in DEP length
Month fixed effects	1 lag in conduct waivers
Calendar year trend	1 lag in QS bonuses
QS bonuses equation:	2 lags in MOS bonuses
UMCSENT Index	
Civilian unemployment rate	
Crude oil prices	
Housing starts	
U.S. leading indicator index	
Recruiters on duty	
Bathtub months difficulty measure	
Month fixed effects	
Calendar year trend	
MOS bonuses equation:	
Relative average civilian to military pay for	
16- to 24-year-olds	
UMCSENT Index	
Civilian unemployment rate	
Crude oil prices	
Housing starts	
U.S. leading indicator index	
Recruiters on duty	
Bathtub months difficulty measure	
Month fixed effects	
Calendar year trend	

Table 5.3
CV Optimization: Phase II

Exogenous Variables	Endogenous Variables
Optimized in this step. Result:	**Fixed in this step:**
CMMGA equation:	CMMGA equation:
Macroeconomic principal component	1 lag in CMMGA
Geopolitical risk measure	1 lag in DEP length
Bathtub months difficulty measure	1 lag in conduct waivers
Month fixed effects	1 lag in QS bonuses
Dummy variable for August 2011	2 lags in MOS bonuses
DEP length equation:	DEP length equation:
Macroeconomic principal component	2 lags in CMMGA
Month fixed effects	2 lags in DEP length
Conduct waivers equation:	1 lag in conduct waivers
Macroeconomic principal component	2 lags in QS bonuses
Adverse events principal component	1 lag in MOS bonuses
Hostile deaths	Conduct waivers equation:
Total deaths	1 lag in CMMGA
Bathtub months difficulty measure	1 lag in DEP length
QS bonuses equation:	1 lag in conduct waivers
Macroeconomic principal component	QS bonuses equation:
Month fixed effects	2 lags in CMMGA
MOS bonuses equation:	1 lag in DEP length
Macroeconomic principal component	2 lags in conduct waivers
12-month lagged MOS bonuses	2 lags in QS bonuses
Bathtub months difficulty measure	MOS bonuses equation:
Month fixed effects	2 lags in CMMGA
Calendar year trend	2 lags in DEP length
Recruiters on duty equation:	1 lag in conduct waivers
Macroeconomic principal component	1 lag in QS bonuses
Adverse events principal component	2 lags in MOS bonuses
Total deaths	Recruiters on duty equation:
Hostile deaths	1 lag in recruiters on duty
Month fixed effects	Training seat as a percentage of target equation:
	1 lag in training seats filled

Model Interpretation

The model presented thus far is quite complicated—it includes a large number of independent regressors, endogenous regressors, and lags. Consequently, interpreting the models is quite difficult. Focusing on the 12-month leading indicator model, for example, the CMMGA equations include endogenous regressors such as a lag of CMMGA and the first and second lag of DEP length; endogenous variables

Table 5.4
CV Optimization: Phase III

Exogenous Variables	Endogenous Variables
Fixed in this step:	**Optimized in this step. Result:**
CMMGA equation:	CMMGA equation:
Macroeconomic principal component	1 lag in CMMGA
Geopolitical risk measure	2 lags in DEP length
Bathtub months difficulty measure	2 lags in conduct waivers
Month fixed effects	3 lags in QS bonuses
Dummy variable for August 2011	2 lags in recruiters on duty
DEP length equation:	DEP length equation:
Macroeconomic principal component	1 lag in CMMGA
Month fixed effects	2 lags in DEP length
Conduct waivers equation:	1 lag in conduct waivers
Macroeconomic principal component	1 lag in QS bonuses
Adverse events principal component	3 lags in MOS bonuses
Hostile deaths	Conduct waivers equation:
Total deaths	2 lags in DEP length
Bathtub months difficulty measure	1 lag in conduct waivers
QS bonuses equation:	2 lags in recruiters on duty
Macroeconomic principal component	QS bonuses equation:
MOS bonuses equation:	2 lags in CMMGA
12-month lagged MOS bonuses	2 lags in DEP length
Bathtub months difficulty measure	3 lags in conduct waivers
Month fixed effects	2 lags in QS bonuses
Calendar year trend	1 lag in MOS bonuses
Recruiters on duty equation:	3 lags in recruiters on duty
Macroeconomic principal component	3 lags in training seats filled
Training seats filled as a percentage of target	MOS bonuses equation:
equation	2 lags in CMMGA
Adverse events principal component	2 lags in DEP length
Total deaths	3 lags in conduct waivers
Hostile deaths	2 lags in QS bonuses
Month fixed effects	1 lag in MOS bonuses
	3 lags in recruiters on duty
	Recruiters on duty equation:
	1 lag in CMMGA
	1 lag in DEP length
	3 lags in conduct waivers
	3 lags in QS bonuses
	2 lags in MOS bonuses
	3 lags in recruiters on duty
	1 lag in training seats filled
	Training seat as a percentage of target equation:
	1 lag in CMMGA
	1 lag in DEP length
	2 lags in QS bonuses
	1 lag in training seats filled

Table 5.5
Goodness-of-Fit by Equation

Equation	RMSE	*R*-squared
CMMGA	0.3693	0.8637
DEP length	0.2713	0.9243
TSFR	0.0626	0.6579
Conduct waiver	0.0066	0.9681
QS bonus	0.0554	0.8974
MOS bonus	0.0315	0.9746
Recruiters on duty	0.0552	0.8581

from Army policy such as conduct waivers, recruiters on duty, and QS bonuses; a composite of exogenous variables from the macroeconomy; a composite measure of adverse factors; and a large collection of time controls.

The main results for CMMGA suggest that macroeconomic principal components have a large and statistically significant effect on recruiting difficulties in the direction we would expect: better economies make it more difficult to recruit. When CMMGA is negative that means the recruiting mission was larger than the number of recruits. An increase in geopolitical risk has a positive effect on recruiting, perhaps demonstrating a call to service due to a necessity for military action.

The endogenous variables are particularly difficult to interpret, owing to the fact that part of the reason they are being turned "on" is that the Army is experiencing recruiting difficulties. For example, the net effect of recruiters, QS bonuses, and waivers in the CMMGA equation are all net negative, owing to the endogencity of these measures. This implies that these variables had the effect of worsening CMMGA (making the recruiting environment worse); however, when the Army deploys more recruiters to the field, uses more QS bonuses, or increases the use of waivers, it is *because* the recruiting environment is difficult. While counterintuitive, this was intentional in the design of the model—essentially the Army has considerable information about recruiting conditions, and that information is embedded in the policies it adopts regarding these policies. It is interesting that the number of recruiters is negative in month $t-2$ and positive in $t-1$. This suggests that additional recruiters are initially placed in recruiting stations when the recruiting environment is very bad, but that once recruiters are in place, the Army is more likely to make their recruiting mission levels. Again, we note that having a lot of recruiters in the field is indicative of a difficult recruiting environment.

The time measures have the direction expected: March, April, and May are all negative, reflecting the importance of graduation from high school and the difficulty of recruiting just prior to the end of the school year.

CHAPTER SIX

Forecast of Army Recruiting Difficulty

Model Validation

With our model optimized to achieve the smallest leave-12-out CV error (CV^{12}), we can use the model to make forecasts. To make a 12-month forecast, we use 12-month lag terms in the optimal specification and estimate it using data from 2003 through 2015. The optimal specification is reported in Table A.1 and Table A.2 in Appendix A. The model parameters are reported in Table A.3. To make 24-month predictions, the same set of variables and lag structure are used, with the exception that the 12-month lags are replaced with 24-month lags.[1] The parameter estimates for this model are reported in Table A.4. When making two-year predictions, the 12-month model is first used to forecast for months 1 through 12 after the last observed month, and the 24-month model is used to forecast months 13 through 24 months after the last observed month.

We conduct both in-sample and out-of-sample validations of the model. Throughout the period of model development, we relied on data from 2003 through 2015. Since that time, we have secured additional data from the Army allowing us to conduct a validation of our forecasts. In Figure 6.1 we present CMMGA (black) and 12-month recursive forecasts (green) starting in early 2012. These recursive forecasts represent the forecasts through 2015 from observed exogenous

---

[1] For simplicity, we used the same sets of variables and functional forms when estimating the models for the 12- and the 24-month forecasts. We used 12-month lag structures in both models because that led to stronger correlations than a 24-month lag structure.

Figure 6.1
Empirical Performance and Current Forecast: CMMGA

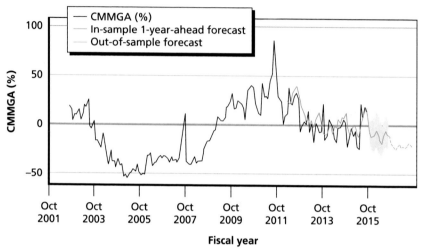

NOTE: The black line in the figure is based on the authors' calculations of CMMGAs using data from the USAREC missioning database and the RA Analyst file. The green line represents a 12-month recursive forecast using the optimized forecast model from January 2012 to September 2015. The solid blue line represents a 1- to 12-month out-of-sample forecast for fiscal year 2016, where the top and bottom bounds of the shaded region reflect the 95 percent confidence interval. The dashed line represents a 13- to 24-month out-of-sample forecast for fiscal year 2017. The CMMGA forecast for FY 2017 is focused on the recruiting environment and does not account for the mission increase of 6,000 accessions that occurred during FY 2017.

indicators and the previous predictions of the model. For example, since the recursive forecast starts in January 2012, the prediction in January 2013 reflects observed changes in the macroeconomic index, adverse events index, geopolitical risk measure, the bathtub measure, and hostile and total U.S. military deaths between January 2012 and 2013. These predictions also reflect predicted changes in the three outcomes and the four endogenous Army responses between January 2012 and 2013 (the observed values for these outcomes are not used). These recursive forecasts are the same that would be used to compute the SOOS PMFE for our optimized model. The 12-month forecasts demonstrate that an in-sample validation of the model does a very good job of predicting a decline in the recruiting environment in mid-2012. The recruiting environment declines (becomes more difficult) and then generally stabilizes from 2013 through 2015. The forecast has a smaller variance than the actual CMMGA and is largely centered on the zero line—indicating that the then-current recruiting environment was neither particularly difficult nor easy.

Using data ending in September 2015 (FY 2015), we generate a 12- (solid blue) and 24-month (dashed blue) forecast from this point. Overall, we forecast that CMMGA will get progressively lower over the next 24 months, indicating that the Army entered a more difficult recruiting environment after FY 2015.

In Figure 6.2, we provide a true out-of-sample comparison of our forecast for FY 2016: the actual CMMGA outcomes (i.e., we did not have these outcomes when we generated the model). We note that the forecast hews very close to the realization of CMMGA for the entire

Figure 6.2
CMMGA: Actual vs. Forecast for FY 2016

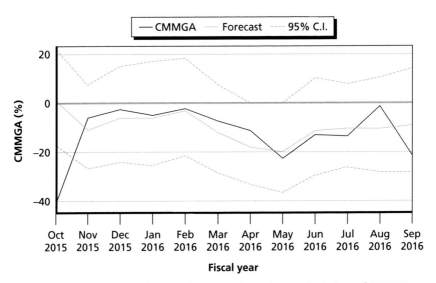

NOTE: The black line in the figure is based on the authors' calculations of CMMGAs using data from the USAREC missioning database and the RA Analyst file. The blue line represents the optimized model's 12-month out-of-sample forecast using only data from March 2003 to September 2015. The dashed green line represents the 95-percent confidence interval for the forecast.

period, with the exception of October 2015. This point was predicted to be much higher. Our prediction was much higher than the observed value owing largely to the high rate of production in September 2015 (20 percent greater production than the requirement). It is likely that Army recruiting pulled in a large number of high-quality recruits at the end of the fiscal year and started the new fiscal year with a significant quality deficit. Importantly, the realization of CMMGA for the entire fiscal year was negative, indicating that the Army was entering a difficult recruiting environment. As a final check, our CMMGA forecast does not systematically under- or overpredict CMMGA. We note that while the fit appears quite good, the error bands are large, suggesting that the 95-percent confidence interval ranges from approximately positive 20 (not a difficult recruiting environment) to −30 (a terrible recruiting environment).

Figure 6.3 shows the analogous results for DEP length. Once again, we see that our out-of-sample forecast compares very well with the realized DEP length. In each month, our forecast is within the 95-percent confidence interval, and the forecast is quite close to the realized DEP length. We note, however, that our DEP length forecast is consistently below the actual DEP length for all but one month (July 2016). Overall, our estimates for DEP length tell a similar story as CMMGA—that the recruiting environment is becoming more difficult. At the beginning of FY 2016 we had a DEP length of nearly 120 days (average DEP length was for a recruit to ship was four months after signing), but by the end of the fiscal year DEP length fell to nearly 90 days. Shortening the average time from contract to ship date indicates that recruiters are having difficulty filling training seats and are relying on shipping new recruits more quickly.

Figure 6.4 presents a 24-month prediction, starting in October 2014 and comparing against the two most recent years of data. The model fits the data very well, with the exception of the shifting of contracts around the end of fiscal year 2015—this caused a surge in mission achievement for September 2015, followed by a shortfall in October 2015. Otherwise, the model tracks the cyclical patterns across the fiscal year, albeit with less month-to-month variance.

Figure 6.3
DEP Length: Actual vs. Forecast for FY 2016

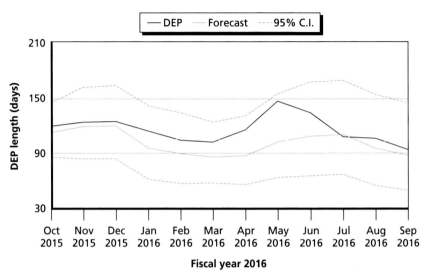

NOTE: The nonflat black line in the figure is based on the authors' calculations of scheduled DEP length at enlistment using contract data from the RA Analyst file. The blue line represents the optimized model's 12-month out-of-sample forecast using only data from March 2003 to September 2015. The dashed green line represents the 95-percent confidence interval for the forecast. The flat black lines at 90 and 150 days represent the lower and upper bound for what the authors consider to be normal DEP length.

Recruiting Difficulty of 12- and 24-Month Forecasts

In this section, we produce our final forecasts of recruiting difficulty. That is, we now estimate the model using all the available data and then use our 12- and 24-month lagged variables to generate the forecast. Since we have data through fiscal year 2016 (September 2016), we will generate forecasts for FY 2017 and FY 2018. In Figures 6.5 and 6.6 we present our forecasts of CMMGA and DEP length, respectively. In addition to the baseline forecast, we provide an additional excursion that takes into consideration that the Army has increased the accession mission for 2017 by approximately 10 percent—from 62,500 to 68,750. Given that the pool of high-quality candidates is relatively fixed, we lower our forecast of CMMGA by 10 percent.

Figure 6.4
Two-Year Validation: CMMGA Actual vs. Forecast for FY 2015–FY 2016

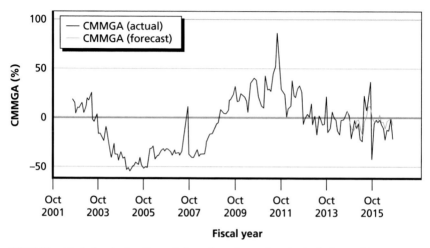

NOTE: The black line in the figure is based on the authors' calculations of CMMGAs using data from the USAREC missioning database and the RA Analyst file. The blue line represents the optimized model's 24-month out-of-sample forecast using data from March 2003 to September 2014.

Figure 6.5
Two-Year Forecast: CMMGA for FY 2017–FY 2018

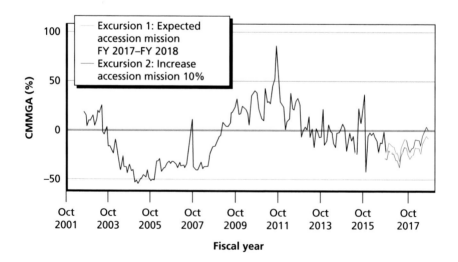

Figure 6.6
Two-Year Forecast: DEP Length for FY 2017–FY 2018

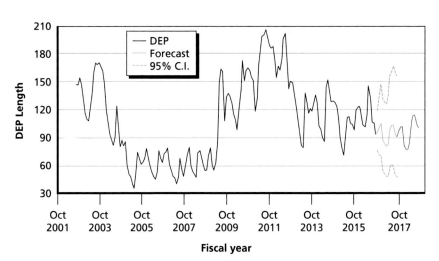

Our forecast of recruiting difficulty suggests that the Army is going to have a difficult time meeting its high-quality accession mission over the next two years. We forecast that the recruiting environment will get worse going from FY 2016 to FY 2017 based on Excursion 1. FY 2016 was already a difficult year (CMMGA was negative in every month for FY 2016) and we forecast that FY 2017 will be worse. Under Excursion 1 (keeping the accession mission the same as 2016) we forecast that CMMGA will average −17.8 percent as compared to a FY 2016 average of −12.3 percent. We note, however, that this interpretation is not strictly correct since it is possible that recruiting missions that follow after a month of shortfalls may be increased to make up for the shortfall. If this is the case, then the end quantity "miss" will not be the sum of the monthly misses. However, the overall measure is at least qualitatively a measure of the size of the miss.

Under Excursion 2 we forecast an even more difficult environment. Using this more realistic scenario, we forecast that by the end of FY 2018 the Army will have had 36 consecutive months of negative CMMGA, an outcome not experienced since FY 2004 to FY 2006.

In Figure 6.6 we present our forecast for DEP length. There is only one forecast for DEP length since it is unclear how to incorporate changes in the accession mission directly into the forecast model. As a consequence, this is likely to be an overly optimistic forecast. The forecast shows a continuation of the decline in DEP length that started in late 2013. While there is a fair bit of cyclicality to DEP length (owing largely to high school graduation) there continues to be a long-term downward trend in DEP length. Examining the FY 2017 and FY 2018 forecasts we can see a number of points where the DEP falls below the 90-day mark. The projected DEP length is not as short as it was in the FY 2004–FY 2008 period, but taken in conjunction with the CMMGA forecast we believe the Army will face a difficult recruiting environment for the next two years.

We note that CMMGA and DEP length together suggest a difficult recruiting environment over the forecast period, and, further, that the confidence bands around our DEP forecast are quite large and suggest that there is some reasonable probability that DEP length will be even shorter and on a par with the FY 2004 period. Conversely there is some chance that DEP length will be in the "safe zone" above 150 days—at least for part of the forecast period. However, since our forecasts of DEP length do not take the increased accession mission into consideration, the probability of a lower-than-forecast DEP is the stronger possibility.

Predictions Beyond 24 Months

Given the DoD program objectives memorandum (POM) budgeting cycle, it is natural for Army planners to want to use the RDI model for predictions beyond 24 months. The model is optimized for 12-month forecasts, so predictions outside of this range exceed its design. However, as we have shown, the model forecasts well through at least 24 months. In lieu of a better alternative, the RDI model can be used to predict recruiting environments beyond 24 months based on a range of assumptions regarding how the leading indicators will evolve in the future. For example, to consider potential recruiting environments, a planner might consider a range of alternative scenarios. Three alternatives include:

1. Return to the long-run average
2. Persistence at the last observed value
3. Persistence in recent growth rate.

The first scenario reflects a notion that long-run economic variables will typical revert to their long-term average (e.g., unemployment rate) over some time period (e.g., a five- or ten-year horizon). The second and third scenarios represent two alternatives for path persistence. What is important is that the planner justifies the assumptions they are making regarding the leading indicators. In some cases (for example, the geopolitical risk index), there may be no obvious reason why it would revert to the long-run mean. In these cases, the second or third alternative scenarios may be a better alternative. Any predictions beyond 24 months should consider a variety of scenarios to test for sensitivity of the predictions to the assumptions being made.

Summary Measures of Recruiting Difficulty

In Figure 6.7 we present a summary measure of recruiting difficulty based on the CMMGA actual data and forecasts, including the excursions discussed previously. To simplify the presentation, we provide an annual average of CMMGA in each year. In the forecast years FY 2017 and FY 2018 we provide two measures, one from Excursion 1 and another from Excursion 2. It is now clear that, under Excursion 2, FY 2017 and FY 2018 are forecasted to be more difficult recruiting environments than FY 2016. We also note that FY 2016 represented the most difficult recruiting environment since before the Great Recession. Additionally, under Excursion 2 we forecast that the recruiting environment could be as challenging as those in FY 2007 and FY 2004. We forecast that FY 2017 will result in a CMMGA shortfall of −25.2 percent under Excursion 2; FY 2007 and FY 2004 had shortfalls of −27.1 percent and −26.9 percent, respectively.

Figure 6.7
Summary of Recruiting Difficulty Using CMMGA

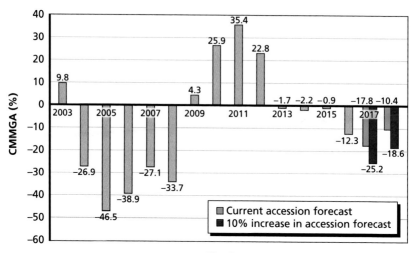

Fiscal year

CHAPTER SEVEN

Recommendations for Leveraging Recruiting Difficulty Index Forecasts

As the difficulty level of recruiting changes in response to changes in recruiting conditions, accomplishing the Army's accession goals requires different mixes and levels of recruiting resources and enlistment eligibility policies. Understanding how recruiting resources and enlistment eligibility policies work together as a system under varying recruiting requirements and environments is critical for decisionmakers who want to use their limited resources to efficiently and effectively achieve the Army's accession requirements. In the last chapter, the RDI model was used to create predictions of the recruiting environment for FY 2017 and FY 2018. Here we consider the implications of these predictions for choosing recruiting resource and enlistment eligibility policies that can accomplish recruiting objectives.

Knapp et al. (2018) developed the RRM. The RRM considers the relationship among the monthly level and mix of recruiting resources, recruit eligibility policies, accumulated contracts, training seat targets, and the recruiting environment. The RRM models how these factors combine to produce monthly accessions and the number of contracts remaining in the DEP at the end of the fiscal year. The RRM and its related optimization algorithm can be used to inform policymakers preparing for alternative recruiting conditions or requirements. It reflects that a more difficult recruiting environment requires either greater resources or expanded eligibility, or both, in order to meet accession goals.

A key input into the RRM is a national measure of recruiting difficulty, which is represented by the 12-month moving average of CMMGA that reflects persistent difficulty in recruiting conditions. We use the predictions from Figure 6.5 to compute the 12-month moving average of CMMGA and use this as an input into the RRM. Using the RRM, we analyze three examples based on a target of a 75,000-accession mission and an 18,750-entry DEP pool for the following year (this is the number of nonaccessed contracts in the DEP at the end of the fiscal year). We will consider the cost-minimizing portfolios required for:

1. An example using RDI's predictions for the FY 2018 recruiting environment
2. An example based on an improving recruiting environment (predicted FY 2018 CMMGA increases by 10 percentage points)
3. An example based on a worsening recruiting environment (predicted FY 2018 CMMGA decreases by 10 percentage points).

We set strict recruit eligibility policies: at least 57 percent high quality, 12 percent waivers, and 3,000 prior service accessions. Additionally, reflecting the FY 2018 assumptions made in Knapp et al. (2018), we assume that there are 12,500 enlistees in the entry pool and 8,800 recruiters on production at recruiting centers at the start of the year; 4.8 percent unemployment (where it was at the start of FY 2017); and prospective TV advertising ranges from $5.6 million to $8 million in April to July, with near zero spending in August and September.[1] Finally, we assume that the training seat distribution follows a pattern that is proportionately scaled up to 75,000 based on the distribution of training seats in the original FY 2017 mission letter.

Table 7.1 reports the costs associated with optimal resource allocation predicted by the RRM using the RDI FY 2018 predictions of CMMGA. Due to the significant accession requirement, costs differ across the alternative recruiting environments in the expected way, with

---

[1]   There is a lagged relationship between TV advertising and enlistment contracts (Dertouzos and Garber, 2003) that the RRM incorporates as part of its contract production.

Table 7.1
Optimal Resource Costs Under Alternative Recruiting Environments: Strict Eligibility

Recruit Characteristics and Recruiting Resources	Predicted FY 2018 Recruiting Environment	Improving FY 2018 Recruiting Environment	Worsening FY 2018 Recruiting Environment
HQ accessions	57%	57%	57%
Waivers	12%	12%	12%
Prior service target	3,000	3,000	3,000
Recruiters (average across fiscal year)	8,984	8,837	9,229
Recruiter costs	$1,060	$1,043	$1,089
Prospective TV ad costs	$321	$294	$354
Bonus costs	$150	$92	$233
Total costs	$1,531	$1,428	$1,676
Accession achieved	99.9%	99.9%	99.9%
Accession + exit DEP Goal achieved	99.2%	100.3%	99.0%

NOTE: The optimal resource allocations are determined by the RRM (Knapp et. al., 2018), which used the RRM optimization algorithm version 1.0. Costs are reported in millions of dollars. The RRM optimizes monthly resource obligations to achieve a 75,000 accession and an 18,750 DEP goal. Key assumptions include: monthly training seats based on the original FY 2017 Office of the Deputy Chief of Staff (ODCS), G-1 mission letter distribution; 4.8% unemployment rate; 8,800 recruiters at the start of the fiscal year; $8M, $5.7M, $8.7M, $7.1M, $0.2M, $0.2M in monthly ad spending prior to fiscal year start (April–September, respectively); and 12.5 thousand entry DEP; recruiting environment varies, as described in text.

the difference between the predicted and improving FY 2018 recruiting environment projected to be a $103 million reduction in annual spending, whereas there is an increase of $145 million annually under the worsening environment.

During FY 2005–FY 2008 (the fiscal years where annual accession goals were 80,000), recruit eligibility was significantly expanded. In Table 7.2, we consider expanded recruit eligibility conditions: at least 54 percent high quality, 15 percent waivers, and 5,250 prior service

Table 7.2
Optimal Resource Costs Under Alternative Recruiting Environments:
Expanded Eligibility

Recruit Characteristics and Recruiting Resources	Predicted FY 2018 Recruiting Environment	Improving FY 2018 Recruiting Environment	Worsening FY 2018 Recruiting Environment
HQ accessions	54.0%	54.0%	54.0%
Waivers	15%	15%	15%
Prior service	5,250	5,250	5,250
Recruiters (average across fiscal year)	8,252	8,261	8,280
Recruiter costs	$974	$975	$977
Prospective TV ad costs	$197	$162	$246
Bonus costs	$20	$20	$27
Total costs	$1,190	$1,158	$1,250
Accession achieved	100.0%	100.0%	100.0%
Accession + exit DEP Goal achieved	99.9%	99.9%	100.0%

NOTE: The optimal resource allocations are determined by the RRM (Knapp et. al., 2018), which used the RRM optimization algorithm version 1.0. Costs are reported in millions of dollars. The RRM optimizes monthly resource obligations to achieve a 75,000 accession and an 18,750 end-of-year DEP goal. Key assumptions include: monthly training seats based on the original FY 2017 other direct costs; G-1 mission letter distribution; 4.8% unemployment rate; 8,800 recruiters at the start of the fiscal year; $8M, $5.7M, $8.7M, $7.1M, $0.2M, $0.2M in monthly ad spending prior to fiscal year start (April–September, respectively); and 12.5 thousand entry DEP; recruiting environment varies, as described in the text.

accessions. In this scenario, required resources are significantly less, and the recruiting accession and DEP goals are uniformly achieved. Conditional on achieving the accession and DEP goals, the difference in total costs is greater between the worsening and predicted FY 2018 environment (approximately $60 million annually) as compared to the difference in total costs between the improving and predicted FY 2018 environment (approximately $32 million annually).

The RRM results suggest that recruiting environment, as measured by CMMGA, can have substantial impact on production ability and costs. Conditional on being able to effectively resource an accession and DEP goal, increasingly difficult recruiting conditions are projected to lead to faster relative growth in costs. In economics terms, this means that recruiting resources exhibit increasing marginal costs with respect to recruiting difficulty. In these scenarios, RDI forecasts can provide policymakers additional time to optimize resource expenditures and to consider expanding recruit eligibility in order to achieve accession goals.

The RRM analysis above highlights several ways that RDI forecasts can be leveraged to aid in Army resourcing and planning. First, it can be used by USAREC as an early warning signal to begin expansion or contraction of the recruiter force and by Army leadership to know when advertising and incentive budgets should be expanded or contracted. Second, it can be combined with the RRM to consider ranges of potential resource costs. Third, it can provide Army leadership with a signal of when the recruiting environment may require expansion of recruit eligibility characteristics.

RDI forecasts provide the Army with a leading indicator that allows recruiting resources and policies to be altered in such a way as to minimize costs while achieving accession goals. If the RDI model is updated and used continuously, it can also help reduce the need to make expensive and stressful changes to the recruiting enterprise that are the avoidable result of reactive policymaking.

CHAPTER EIGHT

Summary and Conclusions

Recruiting resources have typically been determined by how many soldiers the Army would like to enlist (also known as the recruiting mission), and resources have been allocated without regard to the recruiting environment. Consequently, recruiting resources may be insufficient when the recruiting environment is difficult (e.g., during low unemployment rates) and overly abundant during periods of easier recruiting. This mismatch is often difficult to correct as providing a rigorous assessment of the recruiting environment is difficult, and as forecasting changes in the recruiting environment means modeling not only macroeconomic and geopolitical risks but also Army responses to perceived recruiting success or failure. Typically, recruiting failure is the tipping point that leads to increasing recruiting resources and a strong indicator of recruiting difficulty. The unemployment rate is often used as a proxy for recruiting difficulty, but the unemployment rate alone has not been a sufficient signal to reprogram resources. In part, this is because unemployment is only part of the reason for a difficult recruiting environment. General economic and world conditions, enlistment propensity, and the demographics of potential recruits combine with specific recruiting goals to make the job of recruiting relatively harder or easier each year.

Currently, there are only limited metrics of recruiting difficulty, and the relationship between these metrics and required resourcing for a recruiting mission is not well understood. Many of the Army's recruiting tools (e.g., recruiters, advertising campaigns) take time to develop in order to become fully productive. Therefore, the Army needs to understand more fully the primary factors in recruiting difficulty, how much each factor accounts for variation in recruiting difficulty, and the relationships among the factors and conditions that influence them. A national recruiting difficulty index would enable the Army to assess the extent to which recruiting difficulty has changed over time, predict the level of difficulty in future years, and communicate future periods of potential difficulty, thereby providing planners time to sufficiently resource the recruiting mission.

This report provides a review of the existing literature to identify the extent to which economic factors, recruiting mission, DEP posture, enlistment eligibility policies, propensity, recruiting resources, and world/Army events associated with public perceptions of the conditions of service have been shown or posited to negatively or positively affect recruiting difficulty. Based on information developed in the literature review, discussions with resource planners, and additional quantitative analyses, RAND Arroyo Center built a conceptual model of direct and indirect influences on desirable/adverse recruiting outcomes. Based on the conceptual model, the research team built an empirical model that provides recruiting difficulty forecasts for up to 24 months into the future.

The study team identified known and potential indicators of the conceptual factors believed to have a direct influence on desirable/adverse recruiting outcomes at the national level. In addition to publicly available information such as economic conditions and news stories, the research team identified Army data providing levels of accession missions, recruiting resources, and DEP levels; Army data allowing assessment of enlistment contract and DEP characteristics, such as recruit quality overall, DEP length, and whether waivers or bonuses were used; and recruiting-related information such as enlistment propensity, the number of contracts written, and the number of recruiters available. RAND Arroyo Center then built a multiequation model that explicitly quantified the magnitude and lead time of the association between each of these indicators and desirable/adverse recruiting outcomes, such as success in meeting the contract mission, DEP length, and the TSFR. Key to building this model was identifying economic, world-event, and Army policy variables that predicted the recruiting environment with a sufficient lead time. Once we identified potential predictors, the study team "optimized" the model by selecting particular lag structures of the endogenous and exogenous variables to minimize the MSFE. The resulting models were used to forecast the recruiting environment using coefficients from multivariate regression analysis of the associations of the selected indicators with each of the recruiting outcomes. The study team built both 12- and 24-month forecasts, where the 12-month forecast uses 12 months of lagged variables, so that each month's forecast uses real data from as recently as one year prior. The 24-month forecast estimates a separate model with 24 months of lagged variables used in the prediction. Since the 12-month forecast error is smaller, the 24-month forecast is only used for months 13 to 24.

The resulting seven-equation model forecasts whether the Army is likely to face a difficult or easy recruiting environment. The first three equations have dependent variables that are measures of the recruiting environment. The first dependent variable is GA enlistee contracts minus GA enlistee contract mission calculated as a percentage of the GA contract mission. We abbreviate this as CMMGA (contracts minus mission, graduate alpha). This measure is positive when the Army is writing more GA contracts than is required by the mission. GAs are high school graduates who have scored in the upper half on the nationally normed AFQT. The second measure is the average number of days spent waiting to ship out for basic training. This time between contracting and shipping is spent in the DEP. When recruiting is difficult, more people flow out of the pool than flow in, shrinking the size of the pool. The third dependent variable is the TSFR; when recruiting is difficult, training seats go unfilled.

The model also has four endogenous equations—endogenous because the dependent variables are resources or policies over which the Army not only has some control but also is likely to reprogram as recruiting difficulty increases. They are: QS enlistment bonuses—extra compensation to get a recruit to accept a vacant training seat; MOS enlistment bonuses—extra compensation for being willing to serve in a difficult-to-fill military occupation; conduct waivers—waivers for previous behavior that otherwise would have been a bar to enlisting; and recruiters on duty.

Using both theory and previous research, we identify a large pool of potential independent exogenous variables allowing us to estimate the models. Using these independent and dependent variables, we systematically search for model specifications that minimize the MSFE. We also allow lagged variables as predictors within equations and across equations. Our goal is to find variables that function as leading indicators of Army recruiting difficulty so that we can use real data to make a forecast, rather than relying on forecasted measures of our key variables. After the model has been optimized, we use the parameter estimates from the regressions to forecast Army recruiting difficulty for the next 12 and 24 months.

The key variables in the final specification are an index of economic factors, an index of adverse U.S. military events, and an index of global threats. The economic factors include the national unemployment rate for 20- to 24-year-old males, the UMCSENT Index, and housing starts. The adverse events include a LexisNexis index of domestic stories on deployments, deaths, health, assaults and conflicts associated with service members or the Army. The last is a measure of global geopolitical instability gathered from international news stories.

We conducted a number of out-of-sample and forecasting tests. The model performs quite well across a broad range of recruiting environments. It successfully predicted the difficult recruiting environment that the Army faced in FY 2016. At the time, FY 2016 represented the most difficult recruiting environment since before the Great Recession. It is important to note that our model has been developed and defined during a period when the Army prioritized meeting its enlistment goals and during difficult recruiting environments when the Army has demonstrated that they are willing to sacrifice recruit quality to achieve the mission. This is explicit in our inclusion of a waiver equation. Should the Army change its priorities (eliminating waivers or eliminating reductions in quality) the RDI performance will decline and would have to be reoptimized in light of the new Army objectives.

Using our data that ends in FY 2016, we predict recruiting difficulty in FY 2017 and FY 2018. Under missioning and resourcing levels consistent with FY 2016, the recruiting environment is predicted to worsen in FY 2017. Under an alternative excursion that reflects a

10-percent increase in the accession goal, as happened at the start of the second quarter of FY 2017, we forecasted that the recruiting environment in FY 2017 could be almost as challenging as those in FY 2007 and FY 2004. In FY 2018, the accession mission was raised to 76,500 (initially it was 80,000 before being lowered partway through the fiscal year). This represents an additional 12-percent increase over FY 2017, meaning that our predictions are likely to understate the true level of recruiting difficulty in FY2018.

Finally, recruiting difficulty predictions can be combined with the RRM developed in Knapp et al. (2018) to inform policymakers preparing for resourcing requirements under alternative recruiting environments. We demonstrate that, for an accession goal of 75,000, a worsening recruiting environment, represented by a 10-percentage-point decrease in USAREC contract mission achievement for GAs, could lead to a $145 million increase in recruiting costs (assuming the efficient allocation of recruiting resources).

Model Specification and Estimated Parameters

This appendix presents the final model design for the optimized forecast model described in Chapter Five. Table A.1 presents the model specification for the outcome equations. For example, for CMMGA, the model incorporates previous outcome measures including the last month's measure of CMMGA and the previous two months' measures of DEP length but does not include the TSFR. In terms of endogenous military responses, the model includes the previous two months' rates for conduct waivers and recruiters and the last three months' QS bonus eligibility rates but does not incorporate MOS bonus eligibility rates. In terms of exogenous indicators, the model includes the macroeconomic index (based on the principal component of the youth unemployment rate, the UMCSENT Index, and housing starts), the global threat index, the prior year's bathtub measure, and calendar month dummies. Additionally, a special indicator was included for May 2011 because it was an outlier in the overall time series.

Table A.2 presents the model specification for the four endogenous Army responses included in the model presented in Chapter Five.

Finally, Table A.3 presents the estimated parameters for each outcome and for the endogenous policy equations in the optimized 12-month leading indicator forecast model, and Table A.4 presents the estimated parameters for each outcome and for the endogenous policy equations in the optimized 24-month leading indicator forecast model.

Table A.1
Model Specification—Outcomes

Factors Included in Outcome Models	CMMGA	DEP Length	TSFR
Outcomes			
CMMGA	L1	L1	L1
DEP length	L1/2	L1/2	L1
TSFR			L1
Endogenous Army responses			
Conduct waivers	L1/2	L1	
Recruiters on duty	L1/2	L1	
QS bonus	L1/3		L1/2
MOS bonus		L1/3	
Exogenous leading indicators			
Macroeconomic principle component indicator	L12	L12	
Geopolitical risk index	L12		
Adverse factor principle component indicator			L12
Total death rate			L12
Hostile death rate			L12
Bathtub measure	L12		
Month dummies	Included	Included	Included
Dummy for 2011m8	Included		

NOTE: L indicates a lag operator; L1 is a single-month lag; L1/3 is 1-, 2-, and 3-month lag.

Table A.2
Model Specification—Endogenous Policy

Factors Included in Endogenous Policy Models	Conduct Waivers	Recruiters on Duty	QS Bonus	MOS Bonus
Outcomes				
CMMGA		L1		
DEP length	L1/2	L1	L1/2	
TSFR		L1	L1/3	
Endogenous Army responses				
Conduct waivers	L1	L1/3	L1/3	L1/3
Recruiters on duty	L1/2	L1/3	L1/3	L1/3
QS bonus		L1/3	L1/2	L1/2
MOS bonus		L1/2	L1	L1, L12
Exogenous leading indicators				
Macroeconomic principal component indicator	L12	L12	L12	L12
Adverse factor principal component indicator	L12			
Total death rate	L12	L12		
Hostile death rate	L12			
Bathtub measure	L12			L12
Month dummies		Included	Included	Included
Year (continuous)				Included

NOTE: L indicates a lag operator; L1 is a single-month lag; L1/3 is 1-, 2-, and 3-month lag.

Table A.3
Estimated Model Parameters (12-Month Leading Indicator Model)

Variables	CMMGA	DEP Length	TSFR	NPS Conduct Waivers	QS Bonus Eligibility	MOS Bonus Eligibility	Recruiters on Duty
CMMGA (t−1)	0.246*** (0.0742)	0.175*** (0.0609)	0.036*** (0.0094)				−0.025* (0.0140)
DEP length (t−1)	0.084 (0.0886)	0.966*** (0.0776)	−0.021* (0.0111)	−0.005*** (0.00155)	−0.014 (0.0172)		0.002 (0.0113)
DEP length (t−2)	0.099 (0.0866)	−0.188** (0.0760)		0.004*** (0.00153)	−0.011 (0.0166)		
TSFR (t−1)			0.535*** (0.0659)		0.016 (0.0692)		0.1380** (0.0581)
TSFR (t−2)					−0.059 (0.0762)		
TSFR (t−3)					−0.009 (0.0686)		
NPS conduct waivers (t−1)	−0.300 (4.247)	−2.784 (1.734)		0.9239*** (0.0330)	−0.449 (0.769)	1.342*** (0.423)	−0.254 (0.802)
NPS conduct waivers (t−2)	2.878 (4.148)				−0.640 (0.907)	−0.644 (0.504)	−0.417 (0.952)
NPS conduct waivers (t−3)					1.029 (0.724)	−0.414 (0.417)	−0.048 (0.734)
Recruiters (t−1)	−0.519 (0.392)	0.110 (0.2820)		−0.004 (0.0071)	−0.081 (0.0683)	−0.070* (0.0391)	0.272*** (0.0769)

Table A.3—Continued

Variables	CMMGA	DEP Length	TSFR	NPS Conduct Waivers	QS Bonus Eligibility	MOS Bonus Eligibility	Recruiters on Duty
Recruiters (t−2)	−0.581 (0.358)			0.00434 (0.0070)	0.084 (0.0698)	−0.033 (0.0395)	0.176** (0.0741)
Recruiters (t−3)					−0.043 (0.0665)	0.140*** (0.0381)	0.345*** (0.0662)
QS bonus eligibility (t−1)	−1.132** (0.448)		−0.052 (0.0867)		0.722*** (0.0808)	−0.046 (0.0433)	0.162* (0.0877)
QS bonus eligibility (t−2)	0.996* (0.552)		−0.0126 (0.0844)		−0.090 (0.0782)	0.105** (0.0433)	−0.242** (0.104)
QS bonus eligibility (t−3)	0.619 (0.422)						0.001 (0.0797)
MOS bonus eligibility (t−1)		0.217 (0.628)			0.061 (0.0641)	0.853*** (0.0395)	−0.254* (0.132)
MOS bonus eligibility (t−2)		−0.186 (0.867)					0.409*** (0.132)
MOS bonus eligibility (t−3)		0.235 (0.621)					
MOS bonus eligibility (t−12)						−0.053 (0.0413)	
Macroeconomic principal component indicator (t−12)	−0.397*** (0.0499)	0.00675 (0.0321)		0.001** (0.0007)	0.021*** (0.0063)	−0.005 (0.0043)	0.012 (0.0084)

Table A.3—Continued

Variables	CMMGA	DEP Length	TSFR	NPS Conduct Waivers	QS Bonus Eligibility	MOS Bonus Eligibility	Recruiters on Duty
Geopolitical risk index ($t-12$)	0.003*** (0.0007)						
Adverse factor principal component indicator ($t-12$)			0.002 (0.0039)	-0.001 (0.0004)			
Hostile military deaths ($t-12$)			-3.202 (5.738)	-1.467** (0.617)			
Total military deaths ($t-12$)			4.650 (5.074)	1.315** (0.562)			0.010 (1.372)
Bathtub measure ($t-12$)	-0.221** (0.0870)			-0.000 (0.0019)		-0.015 (0.0128)	
February indicator	0.197 (0.138)	0.339*** (0.117)	-0.0324 (0.0267)		.000 (0.0281)	.000 (0.0133)	0.020 (0.0256)
March indicator	-0.061 (0.140)	0.297*** (0.114)	-0.0213 (0.0289)		-0.002 (0.0284)	-0.013 (0.0135)	0.053* (0.0274)
April indicator	-0.028 (0.136)	0.475*** (0.114)	-0.087*** (0.0288)		-0.000 (0.0268)	-0.019 (0.0132)	0.071*** (0.0268)
May indicator	-0.175 (0.135)	0.797*** (0.114)	0.010 (0.0301)		-0.039 (0.0281)	-0.010 (0.0131)	0.077*** (0.0279)
June indicator	0.294** (0.136)	0.582*** (0.116)	0.101*** (0.0284)		-0.024 (0.0273)	0.004 (0.0132)	0.015 (0.0263)

Table A.3—Continued

Variables	CMMGA	DEP Length	TSFR	NPS Conduct Waivers	QS Bonus Eligibility	MOS Bonus Eligibility	Recruiters on Duty
July indicator	0.127 (0.132)	0.487*** (0.111)	0.00342 (0.0263)		-0.012 (0.0256)	0.004 (0.0134)	0.068*** (0.0253)
August indicator	0.329** (0.135)	0.212* (0.110)	0.00105 (0.0262)		0.037 (0.0266)	-0.007 (0.0137)	0.067** (0.0264)
September indicator	0.332** (0.135)	0.333*** (0.115)	-0.0549** (0.0270)		0.015 (0.0251)	-0.018 (0.0133)	0.019 (0.0263)
October indicator	-0.0816 (0.134)	0.534*** (0.114)	0.0610** (0.0289)		-0.031 (0.0261)	-0.020 (0.0135)	0.042 (0.0273)
November indicator	-0.128 (0.132)	0.536*** (0.111)	0.00921 (0.0270)		0.003 (0.0248)	-0.018 (0.0138)	0.062** (0.0251)
December indicator	-0.005 (0.131)	0.495*** (0.110)	0.125*** (0.0266)		0.022 (0.0255)	-0.020 (0.0134)	0.016 (0.0251)
May 2011 indicator	0.910*** (0.311)						
Year (continuous)						-0.005* (0.0027)	
Constant	-0.114 (0.195)	-0.409*** (0.148)	-0.060*** (0.0222)	0.003 (0.00293)	0.070* (0.0369)	9.491* (5.525)	0.081** (0.0384)
Observations	158	158	158	158	158	158	158
R-squared	0.897	0.921	0.623	0.964	0.887	0.972	0.852

Table A.4
Estimated Model Parameters (24-Month Leading Indicator Model)

Variables	CMMGA	DEP Length	TSFR	NPS Conduct Waivers	QS Bonus Eligibility	MOS Bonus Eligibility	Recruiters on Duty
CMMGA $(t-1)$	0.553*** (0.0687)	0.163*** (0.0596)	0.0390*** (0.00960)				-0.0483*** (0.0128)
DEP length $(t-1)$	0.117 (0.104)	0.935*** (0.0758)	-0.0220* (0.0115)	-0.00488*** (0.00150)	-0.00595 (0.0163)		-0.00487 (0.0107)
DEP length $(t-2)$	0.0396 (0.104)	-0.190** (0.0750)		0.00363** (0.00149)	0.00376 (0.0160)		
TSFR $(t-1)$			0.498*** (0.0676)		0.0780 (0.0655)		0.0519 (0.0547)
TSFR $(t-2)$					-0.0873 (0.0697)		
TSFR $(t-3)$					-0.00598 (0.0631)		
NPS conduct waivers $(t-1)$	-4.217 (4.973)	-3.109* (1.640)		0.918*** (0.0342)	-0.620 (0.724)	1.319*** (0.409)	-0.706 (0.735)
NPS conduct waivers $(t-2)$	3.768 (4.845)				-0.693 (0.857)	-0.713 (0.507)	0.321 (0.890)
NPS conduct waivers $(t-3)$					1.205* (0.661)	-0.786* (0.424)	-0.337 (0.679)
Recruiters $(t-1)$	0.269 (0.482)	-0.0252 (0.301)		-0.00513 (0.00708)	-0.0665 (0.0680)	-0.0688* (0.0408)	0.225*** (0.0756)

Table A.4—Continued

Variables	CMMGA	DEP Length	TSFR	NPS Conduct Waivers	QS Bonus Eligibility	MOS Bonus Eligibility	Recruiters on Duty
Recruiters (t–2)	-0.706 (0.436)			0.00464 (0.00708)	0.0531 (0.0694)	-0.0566 (0.0413)	0.0988 (0.0719)
Recruiters (t–3)					-0.0710 (0.0627)	0.161*** (0.0405)	0.404*** (0.0627)
QS bonus eligibility (t–1)	-2.062*** (0.495)		-0.0434 (0.0832)		0.654*** (0.0766)	-0.0344 (0.0409)	0.235*** (0.0809)
QS bonus eligibility (t–2)	1.514** (0.622)		0.0225 (0.0827)		-0.146** (0.0729)	0.100** (0.0419)	-0.253*** (0.0940)
QS bonus eligibility (t–3)	-0.141 (0.476)						0.0987 (0.0735)
MOS bonus eligibility (t–1)		0.0935 (0.600)			0.140** (0.0600)	0.806*** (0.0394)	-0.289** (0.120)
MOS bonus eligibility (t–2)		-0.0899 (0.827)					0.407*** (0.121)
MOS bonus eligibility (t–3)		0.302 (0.591)					
MOS bonus eligibility (t–12)						0.0438 (0.0390)	
Macroeconomic principle component indicator (t–12)		-0.00923 (0.0335)		0.000888 (0.000672)	0.0456*** (0.00721)		-0.0176** (0.00895)

Table A.4—Continued

Variables	CMMGA	DEP Length	TSFR	NPS Conduct Waivers	QS Bonus Eligibility	MOS Bonus Eligibility	Recruiters on Duty
Macroeconomic principle component indicator (t–24)	-0.00702 (0.0516)					0.00610 (0.00513)	
Geopolitical risk index (t–12)	-0.00179** (0.000831)						
Adverse factor principle component indicator (t–12)				-0.000505 (0.000466)			
Adverse factor principle component indicator (t–24)			0.000827 (0.00399)				
Hostile military deaths (t–12)				-1.825*** (0.605)			
Hostile military deaths (t–24)			8.975 (5.470)				
Total military deaths (t–12)				1.688**** (0.559)			0.169 (1.262)
Total military deaths (t–24)			-6.876 (4.698)				
Bathtub measure (t–12)				-0.000208 (0.00192)			
Bathtub measure (t–24)	-0.240** (0.106)					-0.0149 (0.0119)	

Table A.4—Continued

Variables	CMMGA	DEP Length	TSFR	NPS Conduct Waivers	QS Bonus Eligibility	MOS Bonus Eligibility	Recruiters on Duty
February indicator	0.189 (0.156)	0.324*** (0.112)	-0.0542** (0.0255)		0.00796 (0.0260)	-0.00123 (0.0128)	0.0141 (0.0231)
March indicator	0.0126 (0.161)	0.286*** (0.109)	-0.0440 (0.0281)		0.0207 (0.0269)	-0.0136 (0.0130)	0.0349 (0.0249)
April indicator	0.0626 (0.155)	0.469*** (0.109)	-0.107*** (0.0281)		0.0214 (0.0257)	-0.0165 (0.0127)	0.0552** (0.0246)
May indicator	-0.194 (0.156)	0.819*** (0.109)	-0.00806 (0.0296)		-0.0119 (0.0271)	-0.00742 (0.0127)	0.0487* (0.0259)
June indicator	0.216 (0.155)	0.567*** (0.111)	0.0841*** (0.0282)		-0.0107 (0.0260)	0.00822 (0.0127)	0.00211 (0.0240)
July indicator	0.117 (0.149)	0.446*** (0.106)	-0.0109 (0.0252)		-0.0279 (0.0240)	0.00602 (0.0129)	0.0721*** (0.0228)
August indicator	0.220 (0.152)	0.207** (0.104)	-0.00628 (0.0253)		0.0410* (0.0244)	-0.00653 (0.0132)	0.0730*** (0.0236)
September indicator	0.170 (0.153)	0.322*** (0.110)	-0.0666** (0.0259)		0.0223 (0.0233)	-0.0156 (0.0129)	0.0482** (0.0236)
October indicator	-0.193 (0.153)	0.530*** (0.108)	0.0367 (0.0278)		-0.0111 (0.0243)	-0.0184 (0.0128)	0.0419* (0.0242)
November indicator	-0.173 (0.151)	0.531*** (0.106)	-0.00789 (0.0263)		0.0158 (0.0232)	-0.0158 (0.0131)	0.0573** (0.0228)
December indicator	-0.0318	0.505***	0.113***		0.0295	-0.0217*	0.0122

Table A.4—Continued

Variables	CMMGA	DEP Length	TSFR	NPS Conduct Waivers	QS Bonus Eligibility	MOS Bonus Eligibility	Recruiters on Duty
December indicator	(0.150) (0.131)	(0.105) (0.110)	(0.0257) (0.0266)		(0.0236) (0.0255)	(0.0129) (0.0134)	(0.0227) (0.0251)
May 2011 indicator	0.772** (0.348)						
Year (continuous)						−0.00414 (0.00257)	
Constant	0.586*** (0.212)	−0.351** (0.148)	−0.0471** (0.0225)	0.00280 (0.00280)	0.102*** (0.0338)	8.362 (5.187)	0.0706** (0.0351)
Observations	158	158	158	158	158	158	158
R-squared	0.864	0.924	0.658	0.968	0.897	0.975	0.858

Detailed Discussion of Data Sources

Military Data

Data on recruiters are collected from a recruiter database maintained by the USAREC that tracks each recruiter's current status and assignment. The file reflects a monthly snapshot of each recruiter, an indicator of the recruiter's center assignment, and an indicator of whether or not the recruiter is on production (versus on leave or other alternative duty assignment).

Data on contract missioning is collected through a contract missioning system used and maintained by USAREC for it to allocate and report contract mission goals and achievements. It records key measures at the recruiting brigade, battalion, company, and center level. The system is populated by USAREC's allocating a monthly mission to each brigade. Each brigade then allocates a contract mission to each of its battalions. Each battalion then allocates a contract mission to each of its companies. Finally, each company then allocates a contract mission to each of its recruiting centers. This system can be used to generate monthly measures of the contract mission at the respective brigade, battalion, company, or center level for key missioning categories, including high school GAs, high school senior alphas, and others (i.e., GED holders or graduates or seniors scoring below the fiftieth percentile on the AFQT). From the missioning and recruiter data, we compute the number of recruiters on production at the center level by summing up the number of recruiters at centers with a positive mission, and we compute the monthly GA contract mission by summing the GA mission assigned to recruiting centers in the 50 states or Washington, D.C., with at least one recruiter on production at the center.[1] Requiring a center to have at least one recruiter and a nonzero contract mission is done to control for the opening and closing of centers, which can spuriously increase the true mission assigned in a month if it is not accounted for.

Data on contracts written and accessed is collected from the RA Analyst file and other information maintained by HRC. The data gathered from this information captures every contract written from fiscal years 2001 to 2016. It reports key measures of these contracts, including when the contract was signed, the recruiter associated with the contract, the cumulative amount and types of any bonuses associated with a contract, educational background and the outcomes of military qualification tests for the recruit, the projected accession date for the contract, and the actual accession date for the contract. From this data, we compute key monthly contract measures, including the average DEP length, fraction accepting of each type of bonus, total contracts written, and contracts written for specific subgroups (e.g., GAs—enlistment contracts where the individual has a high school diploma and scores in the top fiftieth percentiles of the AFQT), and fractions of NPS accessions with medical, conduct, drug, or administrative waivers.[2] In computing these measures, we again limit the sample to contracts written at centers with a nonzero contract mission in the 50 states or Washington, D.C., with at least one recruiter on production at the recruiting center. This sample selection reflects that the model presented in Chapter Three relies on national measures meant to capture the economic activity in the 50 states and Washington, D.C.

Data on training seats available and filled are collected from the Army Training Requirements and Resources System (ATRRS), a training seat management system maintained by the TRADOC. ATRRS tracks the number of training seats available and the number of train-

---

[1]   In some fiscal years, the recording of missioning at the center level is inconsistent. In these cases, we use missioning at the company level.

[2]   This included waivers at the time of contracting (i.e., DEP waivers) and waivers at the time of accession.

ing seats filled for BCT or OSUT.[3] From this system, we compute the monthly total number of training seats available and filled for BCT or OSUT.

Data on the total training seats planned for future months is collected from the accession mission letter issued by the Office of the Deputy Chief of Staff of the Army (G-1). The mission letter represents strategic guidance to USAREC and TRADOC, reflecting the number of accessions they should plan by month during the fiscal year. The mission letter specifies the high-quality and overall accession targets. It does not divide the monthly accession mission by military occupational specialty and so may differ from the numbers provided in ATRRS. Since the quality targets in the mission letter rarely change across months, we use only the accession mission. The mission letter is released at least once a year to set the next fiscal year targets. If the overall accession mission changes, or if projected accessions exceed or fall short of the original fiscal year targets, then a new mission letter may be released updating the monthly targets. We use the monthly accession mission to measure total training seats planned for future months, which is used in the computation of the bathtub measure described in Chapter Three.

Finally, data on Basic Military Pay came from the Defense Finance Accounting Service, which provides a historical record of the Basic Pay tables. Basic Pay tables generally correspond to calendar years, although some non-January pay raises did occur between 2002 and 2016. The measure for Basic Pay used for calculating the ratio of civilian to military pay was that of an E-4 with four years of service. This was meant to reflect a potential enlistee's perceived compensation if they were to enlist and serve out a complete enlistment term.[4]

---

[3] All soldiers with NPS must go through either BCT or OSUT. OSUT combines BCT with AIT in one location; it is only available for a subset of the military occupational specialties. Depending on how long it has been since they left the military and whether or not they are returning to the same occupational specialty, soldiers with prior service may have to repeat BCT and AIT or OSUT. Most do not need to do so.

[4] Service members receive a number of nontaxable pays that increase their current level of compensation in a way that is not common in the civilian sector. A separate measure was also

National Economic and Demographic Data

Unemployment rates are measured using the Current Population Survey, a household survey administered on a monthly basis by the U.S. Census Bureau, and reflects the official definition of unemployment for reporting purposes. This includes all jobless persons who are available to take a job and have actively sought work in the past four weeks.

Crude oil prices reflect the price of West Texas Intermediate crude oil. This represents the price of "crude stream produced in Texas and southern Oklahoma, which serves as a reference or 'marker' for pricing a number of other crude streams and which is traded in the domestic spot market at Cushing, Oklahoma" (U.S. Energy Information Administration, 2017b).

Housing starts reflect the total number of new privately owned housing units started. This number is based on projections from the monthly Survey of Construction and the Building Permits Survey, which is collected by the U.S. Census Bureau.

The UMCSENT Index is a consumer confidence index published monthly by the University of Michigan. Each month, at least 500 telephone interviews are conducted of a continental U.S. sample (Alaska and Hawaii are excluded). Each survey respondent is asked 50 core questions that are meant to gauge their opinion on their retrospective and prospective personal situation (e.g., "Would you say that you [and your family living there] are better off or worse off financially than you were a year ago?"), expectations about prices and income (e.g., "Generally speaking, do you think now is a good or bad time for people to buy major household items?"), and demographics of the survey respondent. From this survey, the University of Michigan uses five of the questions to create a composite index. As demonstrated in Chapter Three, the inverse of the consumer sentiment index is strongly correlated with CMMGA one year in the future.

---

considered, known as Regular Military Compensation, which accounts for special pays and their tax advantage. The choice of compensation did not prove to be meaningfully important. This is likely because compensation changes occur only annually and hence are hard to identify independently from other cyclical changes.

The leading index of the United States represents an aggregated measure of the leading indexes of all 50 states produced by the Federal Reserve Bank of Philadelphia. The Federal Reserve Bank of Philadelphia describes each state's leading index as based on the state's current index and on other variables that lead the economy, including "state-level housing permits (1 to 4 units), state initial unemployment insurance claims, delivery times from the Institute for Supply Management (ISM) manufacturing survey, and the interest rate spread between the 10-year Treasury bond and the 3-month Treasury bill" (Federal Reserve Bank of Philadelphia, 2017).

National Military-Related Measures

Measures of adverse events in the news are based on historical keyword searches from an archive of AP news stories through September 2013 and then LexisNexis searches of those keywords after September 2013. We record five key categories of search terms: deployments, injuries and deaths, medical support and well-being, military crime and improprieties, and mentions of Middle Eastern conflicts. For each category, the event measure reflects the number of monthly news articles from the AP satisfying at least one of the keywords. For example, the measure for deployments captures all AP articles that reference deployment and also reference the U.S. Army or the U.S. military.

Counts of military-related deaths are collected from the iCasualties database, which tracks service related deaths and whether or not the cause of death was related to a hostile action (e.g., hostile fire). We considered measures of total and hostile deaths as part of the analysis.

Finally, Caldara and Iacoviello (2018) construct a measure of geopolitical risk by counting in 11 international newspapers the number of articles mentioning phrases related to geopolitical tensions. This methodology takes a broader approach than our adverse events measure by focusing more on broad risks, tensions, and threats.

Remaining Technical Notes

In general, data were collected so that they would correspond to the recruiting resources, enlistment eligibility policies, and economic conditions in effect as of each calendar month from August 2002 until September 2016. This covers the entirety of the Army's fiscal years from FY 2003 to FY 2016, as well as the last two months of FY 2002. However, not all data neatly correspond to calendar months. Contract-related measures correspond to recruiting contract months (RCM), which typically run from the middle of the prior month to the middle of the current month (e.g., the May 2017 RCM runs from April 14 to May 11). Starting in 2014, USAREC changed this terminology to "phaseline"; however, we retain the original terminology in this report. Accession-related measures correspond to recruiting ship months (RSM). The RSM ends on the last business day preceding the last Monday of the month, except in September, when it corresponds to the last day of the fiscal year. The end of a RSM typically falls between the end of a recruiting contract month (RCM) and the end of a calendar month. This difference in timing is unavoidable, as some measures are only recorded using one type of month measure. For example, contract mission is only allocated at the RCM level. Likewise, national economic measures are reported at the calendar month level and typically reflect outcome measures from surveys administered over the course of that month. The modeling method described in Chapter Five will consider a variety of specifications that account for lagged effects from key measures of broad economic and Army-specific data.

All exogenous variables that are measured with gaps across months are interpolated using a cubic spline. For example, in most years no BCT begins during the month of December. This institutional detail might bias the measurement of our model, so we alternatively impute a measure of training seats filled. If this were not done, then every December would have to be excluded from our data, and an indicator for each December is not sufficient to account for this effect. Excluding December is not ideal because it is still an important month for writing contracts despite no one starting BCT.

Instructions for Incorporating New Data and Making Forecasts

Document Overview

The main objective of this document is to summarize the steps involved in updating the RDI analysis. The RDI analysis is done at the national-month level. There are five main steps involved:

1. Extract and prepare military data
2. Extract and prepare national economic and demographic data
3. Extract and prepare national military-related data
4. Combine the separate data files to create the main analytic file
5. Run programs to update the RDI analysis.

The following sections are organized by each of the five main steps. Each section will be organized by:

1. Data overview
2. List of variables that needs to be extracted/updated
3. Description of the step
4. Instructions on how to operationalize the step.

Step 1: Extract and Prepare Military Data

Data and Step Overview
In this section, the analytic file draws from five sources of U.S. Army data: data on recruiters from USAREC, data on contract missions from USAREC, data on accession missions from the G-1 mission letter, data

on characteristics of contracts from RA Analyst files, and data on Initial Entry Training (IET) from ATRRS.

The recruiter data includes personnel data, such as job titles, strength codes, and service types. Each recruiter data pull includes historical and updated information.

The contract mission data includes data on quality and service types of contract missions. Each contract mission data pull only includes updated information.

The accession mission data includes data on accession mission goals. This information will need to be input by hand by using PDF accession mission letters from G-1.

The contracts data includes administrative data, such as contract demographics, bonus information, waiver types, accession dates, and quality and service types. Each contract data pull includes historical and updated information.

The accession mission information comes from Mission Letter Memorandums and contains mission goals at the national-month level. The letters are delivered at least once before the start of the fiscal year and are reissued as accession goals change.

The ATRRS data includes data on planned training seats for a given course, class inputs, course phase, class location, etc., for all IET classes from in FY 2000 to present at the class level. This data is directly downloaded from four different ATRRS reports available from the ATRRS website.

First, the recruiter and contract mission data are used to identify centers and months that are active and operating in the 50 states and Washington, D.C., to guarantee that the analytic variables created in this section are for the sample of interest (i.e., recruiting centers with nonzero mission and on-duty recruiters). We then aggregate recruiter and contract mission data to the national-month level. We use the same indicators to identify centers and months that are active and operating in the 50 states and Washington, D.C., in RA Analyst to aggregate data on contracts to the national-month level. Next, we create a "bathtub" measure, which reflects the average fill rate for training seats as of three months prior using accession mission letters and actual accessions from RA Analyst. Lastly, we use ATRRS data and aggregate all planned training seats and inputs for all BCT and OSUT classes to the national-month level in order to calculate the percentage difference between planned training seats and inputs.

List of Variables

The variables that are generated from these four files that go into the analytic file used in the model are:

- Number of on-duty recruiters (recruit_duty)
- Number of GA contract missions (mission_ga)
- Number of GA contracts minus GA contract mission, as a percentage of GA contract mission (cmmga)
- Number of all contracts (contracts_overall_rcm)
- Number of NPS contracts (nps_contracts_rsm)
- Average scheduled DEP (sch_dep_avg_overall)
- Number of NPS conduct waivers (nps_conduct_ad_rsm)
- Eligibility of any MOS bonuses (eligibility_rcm_m_any_overall)
- Eligibility of any QS bonuses (eligibility_rcm_q_any_overall)
- Average fill rate three months prior to "bathtub" months (bt3)
- Number of planned training seats (current_quota)
- Number of trainees who showed up (inputs)
- Percent difference of planned training seats and inputs (totals_per_diff).

Description of Step

In order to update the variables listed above, the steps involve data cleaning of the four files and the identification of recruiting centers and months that are active and operating in the 50 states and Washington, D.C.

Recruiter File

The recruiter file includes personnel data on characteristics of all recruiters at a given RSM. The recruiter data is recorded at the recruiter Social Security Number (SSN)[1] and RSM. In the event of duplicate

---

[1] RAND uses a unique identifier in place of the actual SSN in all files.

observations of SSN and RSM, we prioritize records associated with the active component, four-digit recruiting centers identification designator (RSID), and strength code equal to "duty" because these recruiters are most likely to be actively engaged in recruiting activity. To deal with duplicates, we drop observations of SSN and RSM that were not prioritized.

Next, we organize service types of RA and U.S. Army Reserve recruiters separately into four job classes: on duty, not on duty, missing, and all other.

Next, we aggregate the total number of recruiters for each job class and service type by RSID and RSM to prepare the recruiter file to be combined with the other three primary data sources.

Finally, we create two indicators for RSID and RSM combinations that have positive on-duty recruiters or not-on-duty recruiters.

In this step, we generate a data set that is unique at the RSID and RSM level, which will be used to generate two indicators that limit the analysis to the sample of interest: (1) RSID/RSM combinations that are operating in the 50 states and Washington, D.C.; (2) RSID/RSM combinations that have both positive missions and recruiters. This same data set is also used to aggregate the total number of on-duty recruiters at the national-month level. We also generate another data set that is unique at the RSID, recruiter, and RSM level, which is used to recover correct RSIDs as of the time of contracting. We use this file to identify the first and last RSM for each unique RSID/recruiter combination in order to generate new observations for each unique RSID/recruiter combination where there were missing RSM. We also expand the first and last RSM for each RSID/recruiter combination. This is only done when the last RSM for a given RSID/recruiter combination does not overlap with the first RSM of the same recruiter at a different RSID. This produces a file that indicates continuous periods when a unique RSID/recruiter combination exists and compensates for timing issues between the RA Analyst and recruiter file.[2]

---

[2] This substep is particularly necessary when centers are being opened and closed. The variable for RSID on the RA Analyst file reflects the RSID when the contract's information was last edited. If the original center where the contract was signed was closed, and a new one

Contract Mission File

The contract mission file includes data on the total number of missions by quality and service type. The mission data comes in Excel format where each updated workbook records mission for a given fiscal year (see file "Orig_Adj_Msns(FY16).xlsx" in the data supplement for an example of the file format). The data are in wide format where each observation (i.e., row) has a unique RSID and the columns are associated with the RCM, service type, and quality. Since each contract mission data pull only includes updated information, we append the update to historical data.

Next, we reshape the file from wide to long so that each observation is unique at the RSID, RCM, service type, and quality level.

Next, we then aggregate number of missions for each service type and quality level by RSID and RCM to be merged with the other two primary data sources.

Finally, we create two indicators for RSID and RCM combinations that have positive RA missions or U.S. Army Reserve missions.

In this step, we generate a data set that is unique at the RSID and RSM level, which is used to generate the two indicators mentioned in the recruiter section. We merge the RSID/RSM recruiter file with this contract mission data set to create the two indicators. We create the first indicator for RSID/RCM combinations that are operating in the 50 states and Washington, D.C., by referring to a list of centers. We exclude centers outside of the 50 states and Washington, D.C., because they operate differently, and not all the requisite economic variables are available for them. We then create the second indicator for RSID/RCM combinations that are active by identifying RSID/RCM combinations that have both positive missions and recruiters. We also identify RSID/RCM combinations to keep that do not have positive mission and recruiters based on the data but appear to fall between two months that have positive mission and recruiters given the same

---

opened, then the RSID might change. This method recovers the RSID where the contract was original signed. The RA Analyst file added a variable for the original contract RSID around 2010; however, to ensure consistency across years, we employ the same method of recovering the original contract RSID using the recruiter file.

RSID. The idea is that we want to keep centers that have actual recruiters assigned and have an actual mission number they need to achieve. This newly generated data set at the RSID/RCM level with the two indicators is also used to calculate the total number of overall contract missions and GA missions at the national-month level.

Regular Army Analyst File

The RA Analyst file includes administrative data on enlistment contracts, such as demographics, dates of contract and accession, quality levels, service types, and bonus information. This file often reflects changes to the contract's information that occur while the individual is waiting to access. We include waiver information in the RA Analyst file in order to examine waiver types at the contract level.[3]

Based on our experience working with this file and from validating aggregate monthly Army statistics, several checks are required to ensure that the contract is assigned to the correct RSID and RCM and where and when it was signed (and hence where the credit would have been awarded for its production). Corrections are most frequently required when the gaps between RCM and RSM end dates are large and when centers are opening and closing. We use the second recruiter data set to recover correct RSIDs in the RA Analyst file. We also merge on the two indicators generated in the previous section to limit the RA Analyst data to our sample of interest.

Next, we ensure that contract and accessions are correctly credited against the appropriate month's mission, by correcting each contract's assigned RCM and RSM from RA Analyst to reflect reported RCM and RSM date ranges. This produces a contract-level file with corrected RCM and RSM dates. This file will be used again with the accession mission data.

Next, we aggregate the number of total contracts, number of GA contracts, number of NPS contracts, average scheduled DEP, number

---

[3] RAND's experience from working with these files suggests that contracts are sometimes signed at periods outside of when the recruiter is listed as on duty at a center. This likely reflects that the recruiter file represents a point-in-time snapshot. Therefore, it may miss within-month changes.

of NPS conduct waivers, and the eligibility of QS and MOS bonuses to the RSID/RCM level.

Accession Goals
Accession Mission

The accession missions measure is created using the "Mission Letter Memorandums" and requires the analyst updating the file to manually fill in the monthly accession missions. The letters are delivered at least once before the start of the fiscal year and are reissued as accession goals change. In order to fill in the accession mission spreadsheet (see file "mission_goals_2016.xlsx" in the data supplement for an example of the file format), the analyst updating the file must account for any updates to the missions as they are updating the file. Each row within the spreadsheet represents a month and year combination (e.g., October 2002, November 2002, etc.). There are seven columns representing months out from the month and year of the row (i.e., zero months out, one month out, . . . , six months out). Zero months out indicates the mission for the year and month in that observation, one month out represents the mission for the next month, and so on. Using the most up-to-date mission letter, the analyst updating the file must fill in the correct subgroup (NPS Trainers, NPS Non-Trainers, and prior service [PS] Trainers), and then sum these groups to get the total mission. It is important to not backfill information in time. For example, if a mission letter is released in December of a given year that changes the mission goals for January and February, the observation for December will show the previous goals rather than the updated goals. Table C.1 shows an example of how a revised mission letter, issued in December, would be reflected in the goals spreadsheet. In this example, the original contract mission for January and February are 2,800 and 5,400, respectively. In December, a new mission letter revises the mission upward to 3,500 and 5,600. Since the table reflects the accession goals in place at the start of a month, December remains the same, but from January onward the goals reflect the greater accession mission. This file is then merged on to the RA Analyst data by the appropriate year and month variables.

Table C.1
Example of How to Update Accession Mission Based on Revised Mission Letter Memorandums

Month	Year	0_months	1_month	2_months	3_months	4_months
Oct	2005	5,000	4,050	0	2,800	5,400
Nov	2005	4,050	0	2,800	5,400	5,200
Dec	2005	0	2,800	5,400	5,200	5,500
Jan	2006	3,500	5,600	5,200	4,900	5,500
Feb	2006	5,600	5,200	4,900	5,500	4,900
Mar	2006	5,200	4,900	5,500	4,900	4,800
Apr	2006	4,900	5,500	4,900	4,800	6,000

Accessions Achieved

The number of accessions achieved is very similar to the accession mission data. Here we look at the projected number of accessions for a set number of months out for a given year and month observation. In other words, for a given observation, the accessions achieved zero months out is the number of people who signed a contract during or before that month and who are projected to access during that month. For one month out, contracts must have been signed during or before the month and year of the observation but are not projected to ship until the following month. This is done for up to six months out. Just like the accession goals, this is merged into the RA Analyst file by the appropriate year and month variables.

Army Training Requirements and Resources System

In order to update ATRRS data on planned training seats and reported number of trainees for each IET class, we choose four reports (LISTRP1, SUP1, SUP3, and XFRCLS). The reports are unique at the fiscal-year school-course-phase level. We limit the data to include only BCT and OSUT classes. BCT and OSUT classes can be identified using "select codes," which are descriptors of various characteristics of the courses. Thus, we first pulled all classes that had a select code of EA (BCT) or EG (OSUT). We also excluded classes in the OSUT category that were split-level classes, in which the class is divided into two phases and taken at two different times. Almost exclusively reverse component (RC) personnel take these courses. We also excluded any case with a select code of E6, EY, or BL. These are re-class, enlisted Additional Skill Identifier (ASI) and temporary duty (TDY) en route courses, respectively.

We show a sample of the data in Table C.2, one row for each class for some OSUT classes. Empty training seats are computed by subtracting INPUTS from CURRENT_QUOTA. For example, looking at the bottom row, there were six empty training seats in the class (i.e., 218 minus 212). There does not have to be any empty training seats, or the number of empty seats can even be negative. For example, in the first row of the table there are 49 more inputs than seats. While the number of trainees showing up can exceed the number of official training seats, ATRRS data can at first be misleading in this regard. What often happens is that a large class is broken up into sections based on optimum class sizes, with ATRRS assigning all the quotas in the first class but with the inputs spread among multiple classes. Therefore, inputs exceeding current quota should not be interpreted as a specific class being overfilled.

Table C.2
Example of ATRRS Data at Class Level

FY	CRS	Current _Quota	Inputs	Start	End	Location	Select Codes	Title
2013	11B10-OSUT	171	220	10/5/2012	1/25/2013	Ft Benning	E4.EG.EH	Infantryman
2013	11B10-OSUT	230	186	10/12/2012	2/1/2013	Ft Benning	E4.EG.EH	Infantryman
2013	31B10-OSUT	218	212	8/2/2013	12/12/2013	Ft Leonard Wood	E4.EG.EH	Basic Military Police

NOTE: This is a fictionalized example meant to demonstrate file layout.

We also include canceled classes because, while no one is trained in such classes, they can be associated with a number of planned training seats that would be important for us to capture given project objectives. This is especially important because ATRRS reports do not automatically include such classes; rather, they are a report option that has to be intentionally selected.

Once all relevant classes are identified, the next step is to sum all the training seats and inputs (which refers to the number of seats filled) for all BCT and OSUT classes, aggregating by the month of the start date of the classes. This step produced 184 values for empty training seats (12 months × 17 years). Table C.3 presents a sample of eight values, four from the year 2000 and four from the year 2016. In addition to showing quotas and inputs, the table shows the difference and the percentage difference (DIFF and %DIFF) as well as the contribution from BCT and OSUT in the right-hand columns.

Table C.3
Example of ATRRS Data Aggregated to Month Level

FY	Mo	Current_ Quota	Inputs	_Diff	% Diff	OSUT Current_ Quota	OSUT Inputs	BCT Current_ Quota	BCT Inputs
2000	1	8,014	7,101	−913	−11.4%	2,020	2,373	5,994	4,728
2000	2	10,049	9,172	−877	−8.7%	2,333	2,449	7,716	6,723
2000	4	10,497	7,960	−2,537	−24.2%	3,382	2,613	7,115	5,347
2000	5	10,043	7,655	−2,388	−23.8%	2,468	1,862	7,575	5,793
. . .	. . .	. . .	. . .	. . .	. . .	. . .	. . .	. . .	. . .
2016	6	8,821	6,400	−2,421	−27.4%	1,781	1,644	7,040	4,756
2016	7	8,057	5,405	−2,652	−32.9%	1,896	1,749	6,161	3,656
2016	8	11,293	8,288	−3,005	−26.6%	1,463	1,418	9,830	6,870
2016	9	10,110	9,383	−727	−7.2%	1,950	1,828	8,160	7,555

Instructions on Step 1

To operationalize the description above, please follow these instructions:

1. Make sure you have the following six files required for update:
   a. Contract mission file for year of update
   b. Recruit file including year of update
   c. Historical RA Analyst file
   d. RA Analyst file for year of update
   e. Waiver file for year of update
   f. Accession mission goals file with historical data and year of update (see instructions below for how to update this file)
2. Open "Step1_run_force_data.do"
3. Update version (line 14)
4. Update directories (lines 17–20)
5. Update file names to match (1) (lines 25–39)
6. Save "Step1_run_force_data.do"
7. Run "Step1_run_force_data.do."

Updating the Accession Goals File

The accession goals file is created using the mission letters sent by G-1, which outline the most up-to-date mission goals at the time of the letters' release. It tracks the monthly accession goals that need to be reached in order to achieve the mission goal. If the goals are updated, a new letter is generated and sent out. The mission goal file takes the information and creates a timeline such that the data reflects the information a recruiter would know in a given month. Figure C.1 shows a sample of the mission goal file.

The first column labeled fy_fymo represents the fiscal year and month for the given observation. This means that 201403 is December 2013, 201404 is January 2014, and so on. The other columns represent the number of months out from the observation month that the column represents: total_0 gives the number of accessions desired in that month; total_1 is the goal for the next month, and so on. For example, in line 172, we have the observation for 201403 (December 2013), where there is a goal of zero for December, 5,980 for January, 5,255 for February, and so on, until the final value of 4,190 in June 2014. This information is pulled from the mission letter released on October 2013, and a snapshot of the exact table is shown in Figure C.2.

Figure C.1
Sample of the Mission Goal File

	A	B	C	D	E	F	G	H
1	fy_fymo	total_0	total_1	total_2	total_3	total_4	total_5	total_6
167	201310	7,070	5,860	7,380	4,350	7,000	0	7,170
168	201311	5,860	7,380	4,350	7,000	0	7,170	6,960
169	201312	7,380	4,000	6,665	0	6,070	5,290	6,735
170	201401	4,000	6,665	0	6,070	5,290	6,735	4,520
171	201402	6,550	0	5,980	5,255	6,140	4,210	5,075
172	201403	0	5,980	5,255	6,140	4,210	5,075	4,190
173	201404	5,980	5,255	6,140	4,210	5,075	4,190	3,665
174	201405	5,255	6,140	4,210	5,075	4,190	3,665	4,916
175	201406	5,520	3,745	4,845	4,225	3,965	5,360	7,375
176	201407	3,745	4,845	4,225	3,965	5,360	7,375	4,700
177	201408	4,845	4,225	3,965	5,360	7,375	4,700	5,800
178	201409	4,225	3,965	5,360	7,375	4,700	5,800	0
179	201410	3,965	5,360	7,375	4,700	5,800	0	5,950
180	201411	5,360	7,375	4,700	5,800	0	5,950	5,700
181	201412	7,375	4,700	5,800	0	5,950	5,700	6,350
182	201501	4,700	5,800	0	5,950	5,700	6,350	5,000
183	201502	5,800	0	5,950	5,700	6,350	5,000	4,850
184	201503	0	5,950	5,700	6,350	5,000	4,850	5,500
185	201504	5,950	5,700	6,350	5,000	4,850	5,500	4,050
186	201505	5,700	6,350	5,000	4,850	5,500	4,050	5,050
187	201506	6,350	5,000	4,850	5,500	4,050	5,050	4,050
188	201507	4,780	5,250	5,010	4,330	6,752	5,304	4,580
189	201508	5,250	5,010	4,330	6,752	5,304	4,580	6,115
190	201509	5,010	4,330	6,752	5,304	4,580	6,115	0
191	201510	4,330	6,752	5,304	4,580	6,115	0	6,367
192	201511	6,752	5,304	4,580	6,115	0	6,367	7,910
193	201512	5,304	4,580	6,115	0	6,367	7,910	4,976
194	201601	4,580	6,115	0	6,367	7,910	4,976	4,272
195	201602	6,385	0	6,480	8,195	5,170	4,420	6,850
196	201603	0	6,480	8,195	5,170	4,420	6,850	4,195
197	201604	6,480	8,195	5,170	4,420	6,850	4,195	4,535
198	201605	8,195	5,170	4,420	6,850	4,195	4,535	6,670
199	201606	5,170	4,420	6,850	4,195	4,535	6,670	5,950
200	201607	4,420	6,850	4,195	4,535	6,670	5,950	5,170
201	201608	6,850	4,195	4,535	6,670	5,950	5,170	4,580
202	201609	4,195	4,535	6,670	5,950	5,170	4,580	0
203	201610	4,535	6,670	5,950	5,170	4,580	0	7,015
204	201611	6,670	5,950	5,170	4,580	0	7,015	6,100
205	201612	5,950	5,170	4,580	0	7,015	6,100	4,830

SOURCE: Authors' compellation from active component accession goals issued in memoranda by the Office of the Deputy Chief of Staff (G-1) between 2002 and 2016.

Figure C.2
Mission Letter Example Table for RA Accession Goals

2. **Active Army Monthly Enlisted Accession Plan.** Monthly and quarterly goals are subject to change.

FY14 Active Army	NPSM		NPS Trainers NPSF		Total		NPS No-Trainers	PS No-Trainers	Monthly Goals		Quarterly Accessions Goals		Annual %
13-Oct	3,200	3,296	800	824	4,000	4,120	0	0	4,000	4,120			
13-Nov	5,332	5,240	1,333	1,310	6,665	6,550	0	0	6,665	6,550	10,665	10,670	17.20% 18.72%
13-Dec	0		0		0		0	0	0				
14-Jan	4,856	4,784	1,214	1,196	6,070	5,980	0	0	6,070	5,980			
14-Feb	4,232	4,204	1,058	1,061	5,290	5,265	0	0	5,290	5,265	18,095	17,375	29.19% 30.48%
14-Mar	5,388	4,912	1,347	1,228	6,735	6,140	0	0	6,735	6,140			
14-Apr	3,616	3,368	904	842	4,520	4,210	0	0	4,520	4,210			
14-May	4,848	4,060	1,212	1,015	6,060	5,075	0	0	6,060	5,075	14,810	13,475	23.89% 23.64%
14-Jun	3,384	3,352	846	838	4,230	4,190	0	0	4,230	4,190			
14-Jul	3,536	2,933	884	732	4,420	3,665	0	0	4,420	3,665			
14-Aug	4,352	3,932	1,088	983	5,440	4,915	0	0	5,440	4,915	18,430	16,480	29.73% 27.16%
14-Sep	6,856	5,620	1,714	1,380	8,570	6,900	0	0	8,570	6,900			
Total	45,601		11,399		57,000		0	0		57,000	57,000		

*No set PS or PS No-Trainer missions; such applicants, only, will be accessed to fill shortage MOSs, according to HRC business rules, which HRC will publish monthly. HRC will adjust PS and PS TEAM requirements as needed.

SOURCE: Office of the Deputy Chief of Staff, G-1, *Fiscal Year 2014 (FY14) and FY15 Army Accession Missions* [Memorandum], Washington, D.C.: Department of the Army, October 23, 2018.

If you follow the column called monthly goals, you will see that the numbers starting in December correspond to the appropriate columns in row 172 of Figure C.1. If you move to row 173, you will see that the same numbers from row 172 still appear except now they have shifted one to the left. This should follow intuitively, as January was one month out from December, but now that we have transitioned to the row for January 2014, its goal is zero months out. The data from Figure C.2 remains the most recent data until a new mission letter was released in February 2014. The newer table is displayed in Figure C.3.

Here we can see that the new goals require a mission of 5,520 in March, while the previous file lists a goal of 6,140 in the same month. We use this new information to fill in the goals starting in line 175 in Figure C.1 (the observation for March 2014). There are two important notes to keep in mind. First, we start using a new mission letter in the first full month after its release. Ultimately, we are concerned with the actions of the recruiters; they will not be able to adjust much, if any, of their actions in the same month that a new mission letter is released—though they can begin planning for future months. Secondly, using the same reasoning, we do not backfill information as it becomes available.

Figure C.3
Revised Mission Letter Example Table for RA Accession Goals

b. Enclosures.

(1) Enclosure 1 – FY14 and FY15 Active Army Accession Mission, paragraph 1. Active Army Monthly Enlisted Accession Plan: Changes made to the mission are highlighted in the table in bold font.

Text

FY14 Active Army	NPSM	NPS Trainers NPSF	Total	NPS No-Trainers	PS No-Trainers	Monthly Goals	Quarterly Accessions Goals	Annual %
13-Oct	3,296		824	4,120	0	0	4,120		
13-Nov	5,240		1,310	6,550	0	0	6,550	10,670	18.72%
13-Dec	0		0	0	0	0	0		
14-Jan	4,784 4,840	1,196 1,210	5,980 6,050	0	0	5,980 6,050		
14-Feb	4,204 4,196	1,051 1,049	5,255 5,245	0	0	5,255 5,245	17,375 16,815	30.48% 29.50%
14-Mar	4,912 4,416	1,228 1,104	6,140 5,520	0	0	6,140 5,520		
14-Apr	3,368 2,996	842 749	4,210 3,745	0	0	4,210 3,745		
14-May	4,060 3,876	1,015 969	5,075 4,845	0	0	5,075 4,845	13,475 12,815	23.64% 22.48%
14-Jun	3,382 3,380	838 845	4,190 4,225	0	0	4,190 4,225		
14-Jul	2,933 3,172	732 793	3,665 3,965	0	0	3,665 3,965		
14-Aug	3,932 4,288	983 1,072	4,915 5,360	0	0	4,915 5,360	16,480 16,700	27.16% 29.30%
14-Sep	5,520 5,900	1,380 1,475	6,900 7,375	0	0	6,900 7,375		
Total	45,601 45,600	11,399 11,400	57,000	0	0	57,000	57,000	

*No set PS or PS No-Trainer missions; such applicants, only, will be accessed to fill shortage MOSs, according to HRC business rules, which HRC will publish monthly. HRC will adjust PS and PS TEAM requirements as needed.

SOURCE: Office of the Deputy Chief of Staff, G-1, *Fiscal Year 2014 (FY14) and FY15 Army Accession Missions* [Memorandum], Washington, D.C.: Department of the Army, October 23, 2018.

In order to update mission goals, obtain the letters that pertain to the next fiscal year (this might include some letters from the previous fiscal year) and fill in the rows as described above. Save your updates to a file called "mission_goals_<year>.xlsx" where <year> is filled in with the update year (e.g., 2017).

Step 2: Extract and Prepare National Economics and Demographic Data

Data and Step Overview

In this section, the analytic file draws from two external sources of data: data on economic conditions from the FRED and data on geopolitical tensions from the Matteo Iacoviello Geopolitical Risk (GPR) Project.

The data on economic conditions from FRED includes unemployment rates, national housing starts, etc. Each FRED data pull includes historical and updated information. The data from the Matteo Iacoviello GPR Project includes data on geopolitical risk and tensions. Each GPR data pull includes historical and updated information.

Step 2 involves generating analytic variables of interest from FRED and GPR and adding these analytic variables to the ones generated by Step 1.

List of Variables

The variables that are generated from these two files that go into the analytic file used in the model are:

- National housing starts (HOUST)
- University of Michigan Consumer Sentiment (UMCSENT) Index
- Unemployment rate for 20- to 24-year-old males (UNRATE20M)
- Index of geopolitical risk (Geo-Political Risk - Middle East [GPRME]).

Description of Step

In order to update the variables listed above, we extract the variables directly from updated FRED and GPR data. FRED data is pulled directly from STATA, and GPR data is pulled from the GPR website.

Instructions on Step 2

To operationalize the description above, please follow these steps:

1. Make sure you have the following two files required for update:
   a. RDI_inputs_`year'.xlsx from STEP 1
   b. Download the most recent GPR data from: https://www2. bc.edu/matteo-iacoviello/gpr.htm (Caldara and Iacoviello, 2018)
2. Open "Step2_run_other_data.do"
3. Update version (lines 13–14)
4. Update directories (lines 17–19)
5. Save downloaded GPR data in directory on line 18 ("Intermediate" folder)
6. Update GPR file name (line 27)
7. Save "Step2_run_other_data.do"
8. Run "Step2_run_other_data.do."

Step 3: Extract and Prepare National Military-Related Data

Data and Step Overview

In this section, the analytic file draws from two external sources of data: data on military casualties from iCasualties.org and data on adverse events from LexisNexis.

Step 3 involves updating analytic variables of interest from iCasualties and LexisNexis by populating the updated information by hand.

List of Variables

The variables that are generated from these two files that go into the analytic file used in the model are:

- Adverse Events
  - Number of AP articles with mentions of deployments (adverse_events_deploy_adj)
  - Number of AP articles with mentions of injuries and deaths (adverse_events_deaths_adj)
  - Number of AP articles with mentions of medical support and well-being (adverse_events_health_adj)
  - Number of AP articles with mentions of military crime and improprieties (adverse_events_assaults_adj)
  - Number of AP articles with mentions of Middle East conflict (adverse_events_conflicts_adj)
- Casualties
  - Number of Operation Enduring Freedom (OEF) casualties (*casualties_total*)
  - Number of hostile OEF casualties (*hostile_total*).

Description of Step

In order to update the variables listed above, we will need to manually extract data from LexisNexis and iCasualties.org and append it to historical data.

Instructions on Step 3

To operationalize the description above, please follow these instructions:

1. Open spreadsheet with historical data for the above variables "adverse_casualties.xlsx"
2. Identify the five sets of search terms that will be used to generate the monthly data for each of the variables listed in parentheses:
   a. Deployments (adverse_events_deploy): (U.S. Army OR U.S. Military) AND deployment
   b. Injuries and deaths (adverse_events_deaths): (U.S. Army OR U.S. Military) AND (casualties OR injuries OR deaths OR PTSD OR TBI OR amputee)
   c. Medical support and well-being (adverse_events_health): (U.S. Army OR U.S. Military) AND (veteran OR health OR climate)
   d. Military crime and improprieties (adverse_events_assaults): (U.S. Army or U.S. Military) AND (assaults OR drugs OR gang OR hate crime OR racial)
   e. Mentions of Middle Eastern conflict (adverse_events_conflicts): Iraq War OR War on Terror OR War in Afghanistan OR Afghan War OR ISIS OR ISIL OR Islamic State OR Syria OR 9/11 attacks OR 9/11 terrorists OR 9-11 attacks OR 9-11 terrorists OR World Trade Center OR Al Qaeda OR Al-Qaeda.
3. Navigate to LexisNexis Academic

   The URL for LexisNexis Academic is: http://www.lexisnexis .com/hottopics/lnacademic (LexisNexis, 2018)

   If you are on-site, your IP will be automatically authenticated. If you are off-site, you may need to travel through your database portal page to access LexisNexis Academic.

   Once you navigate to LexisNexis Academic, you should see the screen represented in Figure C.4.

Figure C.4
LexisNexis Entry Page

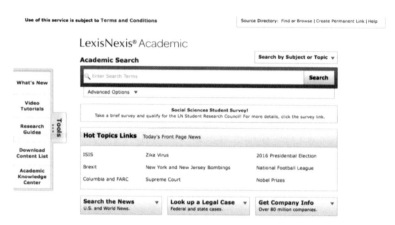

SOURCE: Copyright LexisNexis, a division of Reed Elsevier, Inc.

NOTE: Screenshot captured in mid-2018. LexisNexis will be transitioning to a new display during 2019. Users should validate previous findings to ensure the new browser works in tandem with the old.

4. Copy and paste the key terms listed in Instruction (2) into the main search box and select Advanced Options. An example is present in Figure C.5.

Figure C.5
Example of Keyword Search Using LexisNexis Advanced Options

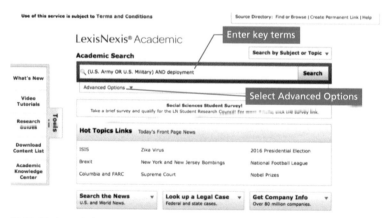

SOURCE: Copyright LexisNexis, a division of Reed Elsevier, Inc.

NOTE: Screenshot captured in mid-2018. LexisNexis will be transitioning to a new display during 2019. Users should validate previous findings to ensure the new browser works in tandem with the old.

5. Select the month of interest. The example presented in Figure C.6 shows the first fiscal month of 2016 (October 2016).

Figure C.6
Example of Month Selection in LexisNexis Advanced Options

SOURCE: Copyright LexisNexis, a division of Reed Elsevier, Inc.

NOTE: Screenshot captured in mid-2018. LexisNexis will be transitioning to a new display during 2019. Users should validate previous findings to ensure the new browser works in tandem with the old.

6.   Select "The Associated Press" as the source; make sure nothing is selected under Content Type and select **Apply.**

Figure C.7
Example of Source Selection in LexisNexis Advanced Options

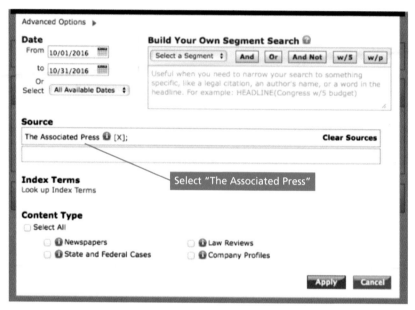

SOURCE: Copyright LexisNexis, a division of Reed Elsevier, Inc.

NOTE: Screenshot captured in mid-2018. LexisNexis will be transitioning to a new display during 2019. Users should validate previous findings to ensure the new browser works in tandem with the old.

7.   Select **Search** once you return to the same screen as Figure C.5.
8.   Turn on Duplicate Options by selecting "On—Moderate similarity."

Figure C.8
Example of Duplication Reduction Using LexisNexis Advanced Options

SOURCE: Copyright LexisNexis, a division of Reed Elsevier, Inc.

NOTE: Screenshot captured in mid-2018. LexisNexis will be transitioning to a new display during 2019. Users should validate previous findings to ensure the new browser works in tandem with the old.

9.   Record total number of search results for this month and variable in "adverse_casualties.xlsx."

Figure C.9
Example of Keyword Search Using LexisNexis Advanced Options

SOURCE: Copyright LexisNexis, a division of Reed Elsevier, Inc.

NOTE: Screenshot captured in mid-2018. LexisNexis will be transitioning to a new display during 2019. Users should validate previous findings to ensure the new browser works in tandem with the old.

10. Repeat Instructions (2)–(8) for all months in time period of interest.
11. Navigate to iCasualties website (http://icasualties.org/OEF/index .aspx).
12. Scroll down to the link at the bottom of the homepage and click on "Fatalities By Year and Month" as noted in Figure C.10.

Figure C.10
Example of Month Selection on iCasualties

Fatalities By Year and Country	**Fatalities By Year and Month**	Fatalities By Country	US Wounded By Year

Iraq

Period	Jan	Feb	Mar	Apr	May	Jun	Jul	Aug	Sep	Oct	Nov	Dec	Total
2003	0	0	92	80	42	36	49	43	33	47	110	48	580
2004	52	23	52	140	84	50	58	75	87	68	141	76	906
2005	127	60	39	52	88	83	58	85	52	99	86	68	897
2006	64	58	34	82	79	63	46	66	77	111	78	115	873
2007	86	85	82	117	131	108	89	88	70	40	40	25	961
2008	40	30	40	52	21	31	13	23	25	14	17	16	322
2009	16	18	9	19	25	15	8	7	10	8	11	3	149
2010	6	6	7	8	6	8	4	3	7	3	2	2	62
2011	7	3	3	11	2	15	6	0	4	4	2	1	58
2012	0	1	0	1	0	0	0	0	0	0	0	0	2
2014	0	0	0	0	0	0	0	0	0	3	0	1	4
2015	0	0	1	1	2	2	0	0	2	1	1	0	10
2016	2	0	2	3	3	0	1	1	3	0	5	0	20
2017	4	1	3	3	1	0	0	5	1	1	2	3	24
2018	2	1	8	2	0	0	2	1	0	2	0	0	18

SOURCE: Copyright iCasualties.org.
NOTE: Screenshot captured in 2017.

Step 4: Combine the Separate Data Files to Create the Main Analytical File

Data and Step Overview

In this section, we combine all data/information extracted from previous steps and generate the analytic variables we use in the model.

Final List of Analytic Variables

Army Variables

- Number of GA contracts minus GA mission, as a percentage of GA mission (cmmga)

- Number of GA missions per one on-duty recruiter (recruit_duty_ alt)
- Average scheduled DEP (sch_dep_avg_rcm)
- Number of NPS conduct waivers (nps_conduct_ad_rsm)
- Eligibility of any MOS bonuses (eligibility_rcm_m_any)
- Eligibility of any QS bonuses (eligibility_rcm_q_anyl)
- Average fill rate 3 months prior to "bathtub" months (bt3)
- Percent difference of planned training seats and inputs (trseat_ perc_diff).

External Variables

- First principal component factor of the economic variables from Step 4 (pc1)
- Average principal component factor of the adverse events variables from Step 2 (pc_av)
- Rate of hostile casualties per contract (hos_rate)
- Rate of casualties per contract (cas_rate)
- Index of geopolitical risk (Geo-Political Risk - Middle East [GPRME]).

Description of Step

In this step, we finalize the generation of variables used in the RDI model by combining data extracted from all the previous steps.

Instructions on Step 4

To operationalize the description above, please follow these instructions:

1. Make sure you have the following two files required for update:
   a. RDI_inputs_`year'.xlsx from STEP 2
   b. Adverse_casualties.xlsx from STEP 3
2. Open "Step4_gen_analytic_file.do"
3. Update version (lines 13–14)
4. Update directories (lines 17–19)
5. Make sure file names to match (1) (lines 25–27)
6. Save "Step4_gen_analytic_file.do"
7. Run "Step4_gen_analytic_file.do."

Step 5: Run Programs to Update RDI Analysis

Data and Step Overview

In this section, we update the RDI analysis by using the updated analytic file generated from the previous four steps.

Final List of Analytic Variables

Army Variables

- Number of GA contracts minus GA mission, as a percentage of GA mission (cmmga)
- Number of GA missions per one on-duty recruiter (recruit_duty_alt)
- Average scheduled DEP (sch_dep_avg_rcm)
- Number of NPS conduct waivers (nps_conduct_ad_rsm)
- Eligibility of any MOS bonuses (eligibility_rcm_m_any)
- Eligibility of any QS bonuses (eligibility_rcm_q_anyl)
- Average fill rate 3 months prior to "bathtub" months (bt3)
- Percent difference of planned training seats and inputs (trseat_perc_diff).

External Variables

- First principal component factor of the economic variables from Step 4 (pc1)
- Average principal component factor of the adverse events variables from Step 2 (pc_av)
- Rate of hostile casualties per contract (hos_rate)
- Rate of casualties per contract (cas_rate)
- Index of geopolitical risk (Geo-Political Risk - Middle East [GPRME]).

Description of Step

In this step, we update the RDI analysis by using the updated analytic file generated from the previous 4 steps.

Instructions on Step 5

To operationalize the description above, please follow these instructions:

1. Open "Step5_run_rdi_analysis.do"
2. Update version (lines 13–14)
3. Save "Step5_run_rdi_analysis.do"
4. Run "Step5_run_rdi_analysis.do."

References

Asch, B., "Cash Compensation for Active-Duty Military Personnel," Santa Monica, Calif.: RAND Corporation, RB-7554-OSD, 2003. As of September 19, 2018:
https://www.rand.org/pubs/research_briefs/RB7554.html

Asch, B., P. Heaton, J. Hosek, P. Martorell, C. Simon, and J. Warner, *Cash Incentives and Military Enlistment, Attrition, and Reenlistment*, Santa Monica, Calif.: RAND Corporation, MG-950-OSD, 2010. As of March 30, 2017:
https://www.rand.org/pubs/monographs/MG950.html

Asch, B., J. Hosek, and J. Warner, "New Economics of Manpower in the Post–Cold War Era," in Todd Sandler and Keith Hartley, eds., *Handbook of Defense Economics*, Vol. 2, Amsterdam: Elsevier, 2007, pp. 1076–1138.

Ash, C., B. Udis, and R. F. McNown, "Enlistments in the All-Volunteer Force: A Military Personnel Supply Model and Its Forecasts," *American Economic Review*, Vol. 73, No. 1, 1983, pp. 145–155.

Brown, C., "Military Enlistments: What Can We Learn From Geographic Variation?" *American Economic Review*, Vol. 75, No. 1, 1985, pp. 228–234.

Caldara, Dario, and Matteo Iacoviello, *Measuring Geopolitical Risk*, International Finance Discussion Papers 1222, Washington, D.C.: Board of Governors of the Federal Reserve System, February 2018. As of September 20, 2018:
https://www2.bc.edu/matteo-iacoviello/gpr.htm

Dale, C., and C. Gilroy, "Enlistments in the All-Volunteer Force: Note," *American Economic Review*, Vol. 75, No. 3, 1985, pp. 547–551.

Dertouzos, J., and S. Garber, *Is Military Advertising Effective? An Estimation Methodology and Applications to Recruiting in the 1980s and 1990s*, Santa Monica, Calif.: RAND Corporation, MR-1591-OSD, 2003. As of September 19, 2018:
https://www.rand.org/pubs/monograph_reports/MR1591.html

Federal Reserve Bank of Philadelphia, *State Leading Indexes*, 2017. As of May 8, 2017:
https://www.philadelphiafed.org/research-and-data/regional-economy/indexes/leading/

Federal Reserve Bank of St. Louis, "Leading Index for the United States (USSLIND)," FRED Economic Data, St. Louis, Mo.: Federal Reserve Bank of St. Louis, 2017. As of May 8, 2017:
https://fred.stlouisfed.org/series/USSLIND

Goldberg, L., "Recruiters, Advertising, and Navy Enlistment," *Naval Research Logistics Quarterly*, Vol. 29, No. 2, June 1982.

Goldberg, L., P. Greenston, S. Hermansen, S. Andrews, G. Thomas, G. Yates, and C. Lavery, *Enlistment Early Warning System and Accession Crisis Prevention Process*, Reston, Va.: Economic Research Laboratory, Inc., June 1984.

Goldberg, L., and D. Kimko, *An Army Enlistment Early Warning System*, Alexandria, Va.: Institute for Defense Analysis, 2003.

Goldberg, L., D. Kimko, M. X. Li, *Analysis and Forecasts of Army Enlistment Supply*, Alexandria, Va.: Institute for Defense Analysis, 2015.

Grissmer, D. W., "The Supply of Enlisted Volunteers in the Post-Draft Environment: An Analysis Based on Monthly Data," in R. V. Cooper, ed., *Defense Manpower Policy*, Santa Monica, Calif.: RAND Corporation, 1979.

Hansen, B., "Multi-Step Forecast Model Selection," *20th Annual Meetings of the Midwest Econometrics Group*, St. Louis, Mo.: Washington University in St. Louis, October 1–2, 2010.

Hosek, J., B. Asch, and M. Mattock, *Should the Increase in Military Pay Be Slowed?* Santa Monica, Calif.: RAND Corporation, TR-1185-OSD, 2012. As of September 19, 2018:
https://www.rand.org/pubs/technical_reports/TR1185.html

Hosek, J., and J. Sharp, *Keeping Military Pay Competitive: The Outlook for Civilian Wage Growth and Its Consequences*, Santa Monica, Calif.: RAND Corporation, IP-205-A, 2001. As of September 19, 2018:
https://www.rand.org/pubs/issue_papers/IP205.html

iCasualties.org: Operation Iraqi Freedom and Operation Enduring Freedom/ Afghanistan, homepage, undated. As of September 19, 2018:
http://icasualties.org

Kapp, L., *Recruiting and Retention: An Overview of FY2011 and FY2012 Results for Active and Reserve Component Enlisted Personnel*, Washington, D.C.: Congressional Research Service, 2013.

Knapp, D., B. Orvis, C. Maerzluft, and T. Tsai, *Resources Required to Meet the U.S. Army's Enlisted Recruiting Requirements Under Alternative Recruiting Goals, Conditions, and Eligibility Policies*, Santa Monica, Calif.: RAND Corporation, RR-2364-A, 2018. As of September 19, 2018:
https://www.rand.org/pubs/research_reports/RR2364.html

LexisNexis, *LexisNexis® Academic*, New York, undated. As of September 20, 2018:
http://www.lexisnexis.com/hottopics/lnacademic/

McElroy, T., and M. Wildi, "Multi-Step-Ahead Estimation of Time Series Models," *International Journal of Forecasting*, Vol. 29, No. 3, 2013, pp. 378–394.

Murray, M., and L. McDonald, *Recent Recruiting Trends and Their Implications for Models of Enlistment Supply*, Santa Monica, Calif.: RAND Corporation, MR-847-OSD/A, 1999. As of September 19, 2018: https://www.rand.org/pubs/monograph_reports/MR847.html

Oi, Walter Y., and Brian E. Forst, "Manpower and Budgeting Implications of Ending Conscription," *Studies Prepared for the President's Commission on an All-Volunteer Armed Force*, Vol. 2, Washington, D.C.: U.S. Government Printing Office, 1971, pp. I-1–1.

University of Michigan, "University of Michigan: Consumer Sentiment (UMCSENT)," graph, St. Louis, Mo.: FRED Economic Data, Federal Reserve Bank of St. Louis, 2017a. As of May 7, 2017: https://fred.stlouisfed.org/series/UMCSENT

University of Michigan, "Index Calculations," *Surveys of Consumers*, Ann Arbor, Mich.: University of Michigan, 2017b. As of May 8, 2017: https://data.sca.isr.umich.edu/fetchdoc.php?docid=24770

U.S. Bureau of Economic Analysis, "Government Social Benefits: To Persons: Federal: Benefits from Social Insurance Funds: Unemployment Insurance: Emergency Unemployment Compensation (B1590C1A027NBEA)," graph, St. Louis, Mo.: FRED Economic Data, Federal Reserve Bank of St. Louis, 2017. As of September 19, 2018: https://fred.stlouisfed.org/series/B1590C1A027NBEA

U.S. Bureau of Labor Statistics, "Civilian Unemployment Rate (UNRATE)," graph, St. Louis, Mo.: FRED Economic Data, Federal Reserve Bank of St. Louis, 2017a. As of May 8, 2017: https://fred.stlouisfed.org/series/UNRATE

U.S. Bureau of Labor Statistics, "Employed Full Time: Median Usual Weekly Nominal Earnings (Second Quartile): Wage and Salary Workers: 16 to 24 Years (LEU0252886300Q)," graph, St. Louis, Mo.: FRED Economic Data, Federal Reserve Bank of St. Louis, 2017b. As of September 19, 2018: https://fred.stlouisfed.org/series/LEU0252886300Q

U.S. Bureau of Labor Statistics, "Unemployment Rate: 20 to 24 years (LNS14000036)," graph, St. Louis, Mo.: FRED Economic Data, Federal Reserve Bank of St. Louis, 2017c. As of May 7, 2017: https://fred.stlouisfed.org/series/LNS14000036

U.S. Census Bureau, "Housing Starts: Total: New Privately Owned Housing Units Started (HOUST)," graph, St. Louis, Mo.: FRED Economic Data, Federal Reserve Bank of St. Louis, 2017. As of May 7, 2017: https://fred.stlouisfed.org/series/HOUST

U.S. Congress, Congressional Budget Office (CBO), *CBO's Economic Forecasting Record: 2017 Update*, Washington, D.C.: CBO, October 2017. As of September 18, 2018:
https://www.cbo.gov/system/files/115th-congress-2017-2018/reports/53090-economicforecastaccuracy.pdf

U.S. Energy Information Administration, "Crude Oil Prices: West Texas Intermediate (WTI)—Cushing, Oklahoma (DCOILWTICO)," graph, St. Louis, Mo.: FRED Economic Data, Federal Reserve Bank of St. Louis, 2017a. As of May 7, 2017:
https://fred.stlouisfed.org/series/DCOILWTICO

U.S. Energy Information Administration, *Petroleum and Other Liquids: Definitions, Sources and Explanatory Notes*, Washington, D.C.: U.S. Department of Energy, 2017b. As of May 8, 2017:
https://www.eia.gov/dnav/pet/TblDefs/pet_pri_spt_tbldef2.asp

U.S. President's Commission on an All-Volunteer Armed Force, *Studies Prepared for the President's Commission on an All-Volunteer Armed Force*, Vol. 2, Washington, D.C.: U.S. Government Printing Office, 1971.

Warner, J., C. Simon, and D. Payne, "The Military Recruiting Productivity Slowdown: The Roles of Resources, Opportunity Cost and the Tastes of Youth," *Defence and Peace Economics*, Vol. 14, No. 5, 2003, pp. 329–342.

Withers, G. A., "International Comparisons in Manpower Supply," in *Defense Manpower Policy: Presentations from the 1976 Rand Conference on Defense Manpower*, ed., R. V. L. Cooper, pp. 116–136, Santa Monica, Calif.: RAND Corporation, R-2396-ARPA, 1979. As of September 19, 2018:
https://www.rand.org/pubs/reports/R2396.html